Ghosts of Alcatraz

Kathryn Vercillo

Schiffer Publishing Ltd ®

4880 Lower Valley Road, Atglen, Pennsylvania 19310

Schiffer Books are available at special discounts for bulk purchases for sales promotions or premiums. Special editions, including personalized covers, corporate imprints, and excerpts can be created in large quantities for special needs. For more information contact the publisher:

Published by Schiffer Publishing Ltd.
4880 Lower Valley Road
Atglen, PA 19310
Phone: (610) 593-1777; Fax: (610) 593-2002
E-mail: Info@schifferbooks.com

For the largest selection of fine reference books on this and related subjects,
please visit our web site at www.schifferbooks.com
We are always looking for people to write books on new and related subjects. If
you have an idea for a book please contact us at the above address.

This book may be purchased from the publisher.Include $3.95 for shipping.
Please try your bookstore first.You may write for a free catalog.

In Europe, Schiffer books are distributed by
Bushwood Books
6 Marksbury Ave.
Kew Gardens
Surrey TW9 4JF England
Phone: 44 (0) 20 8392-8585; Fax: 44 (0) 20 8392-9876
E-mail: info@bushwoodbooks.co.uk
Website: www.bushwoodbooks.co.uk
Free postage in the U.K., Europe; air mail at cost.

Other Schiffer Books by Kathryn Vercillo
Ghosts of San Francisco, 978-0-7643-2765-0, $14.95

Other Schiffer Books on Related Subjects
California Ghosts, 0-7643-1972-8, $14.95
UFOs Over California, 0-7643-2149-8, $14.95
Supernatural California, 0-7643-2401-2, $24.95
Schiffer Publishing has a wide variety of books about ghosts and supernatural happenings. Please visit our website for more great titles.

Designed by Stephanie Daugherty
Type set in Burton's Nightmare 2000/Arrus BT
ISBN: 978-0-7643-2884-8
Printed in China

Dedication

This book is dedicated to my family for their unflagging support of everything that I do. It is dedicated to the friends who will read it although they wouldn't if anyone had written it but me. It is dedicated to my business partner who put up with my lack of productivity during the time it was being written. And it's dedicated to my photographer, who helped me to see the island – and the rest of life – through a new lens.

Contents

PART V: Your Trip To Alcatraz

Introduction

Just over a mile away from the city of San Francisco sits Alcatraz Island. Its rich history includes eras as a military fort, a federal prison, and a center for Native American activist occupation. Today Alcatraz is a tourist attraction for visitors of the Bay Area.

The small island of Alcatraz has captured the interest of travelers from across the globe since the time that the San Francisco Bay Area was first developed. Perhaps it's the way in which the island is almost always enshrouded in a thick layer of ethereal fog. Maybe it's the proximity of the lonely island to the bustling city of San Francisco and the discrepancy between the lives lived in each of those close but separate locations. Certainly, it is something that has been enhanced over time as history has added reason after reason for additional stories to come flowing out of the island's existance.

The rich and complex history of the island is one that incorporates the painful stories of tragic lives lived over a long period of time. The Spanish explorers first "discovered" the island in the sixteenth century, but of course there were Native American settlers in the Bay Area at that time who already knew of the island's existence. Although they could see it, they stayed away from it, because even then...the place had a menacing air to it. Eventually, people did come to inhabit the island. As both a military and federal prison, the island of Alcatraz housed those members of society whose lives, for one reason or another, took a turn for the worse and placed them in the confines of high-security in-carceration. The torture and pain of a life lived in an island prison was conducive to the prevailing tragedy that lingers there even today. Later, the Native American people finally did inhabit the island in an ongoing protest that lasted for more than a year — and although the ending was not exactly tragic, it was not a happy tale either.

Today the island of Alcatraz sits comfortably in the San Francisco Bay, maintained by the United States National Park Service, and is visited daily by boats filled with tour-ists interested in satiating their endless curiosity for the history and tales of this area attraction. But despite the talkative explanations of tour guides, the laughter of travel-ing children echoing throughout the buildings, the modern technology used for island tours, and the beautiful plant life maintained by volunteers, the island of Alcatraz still reeks of the horrors of its past.

And many argue that this past is a past that is simply not going to go away. Travelers visiting Alcatraz today, and those people who once worked on the island or who were incarcerated there during the active history of the federal prison, have regularly reported spirit activity on the small island. Surely, some of the tales are fictional and many are probably exaggerated — the setting and ambience of the island are naturally conducive to fanciful enhancements of the imagination. The constant chill, the strange sounds, and the eerie feelings held there—simply by virtue of the

dilapidation of the old buildings—all make it easy to believe that there are spirits where perhaps there are not. But
mingled within the possible fantasies and tall tales, there
are experiences of ghosts on Alcatraz Island that seem just
a little too eerie to be made up and which are repeated
often enough by others to give them that ring of truth that
makes you wonder just what is happening on the darker
side of the island.

It is impossible to extract the truth from fiction when
talking about Alcatraz. This is because the secrecy surrounding the island's controversial history, the exaggerations and
untruths about the island printed by the media over time,
and the general lack of consistency in reporting the area's
history combine together to create a story that is filled with
confusion. But this inability to distinguish the details of
the island's sordid past is part of what makes Alcatraz as
magical as it is. The prisoners of Alcatraz may have worn
the traditional stripes of black and white, but the history of
Alcatraz can only be told in shades of grey—shades that are
sometimes as thick and impenetrable as the Bay Area fog
that permeates the area around the island. And it is these
shades of grey that makes Alcatraz an area where ghost
stories are bound to thrive.

Ghosts of Alcatraz makes little attempt to separate fact
from fiction. Although extensive research went into the writing of this book, it would be impossible to sort out all of the
truths from all of the half-truths and untruths that exist in
a history as rich and complex as that of this incarceration
island. Instead, this book shares the tales of the area with
you and allows you to determine for yourself what level of
truth you want to take away from the story.

For this reason, you can use *Ghosts of Alcatraz* in whatever way you see fit. If you are a fan of military history,
Bay Area history, or the history of prisons in general, you
will find a plethora of information here that you can add to
your arsenal of knowledge about those topics. If you are a

ghost-hunter interested in learning more about the haunted areas of Alcatraz, you will find that the maps showing the history of hauntings and the tales re-told here will give you a strong starting point for exploring the stories of the spirits that are said to linger on the island. And if you're merely a traveler with an interest in seeing another side of San Francisco—a darker side that sits so close to the beauty of the Golden Gate Bridge and the rich culture and nightlife of the city itself—you should find that *Ghosts of Alcatraz* takes you into the history and present life on the island in a way that isn't experienced within the city itself.

At the conclusion of this book, you may find that you believe that the famous prisoners who haunt these pages are still lingering around the Bay Area today. Or you may find that you've simply learned a lot about the history of how these people lived when they were alive. But undoubtedly, you will find that any trip you take to Alcatraz Island will be different from how it was before you knew what you know after learning about this area. The final chapters of *Ghosts of Alcatraz* will provide you with the information that you need to make the most of your experience at Alcatraz … so you can get your gear ready, prepare yourself for the mystery, and book those tickets. That is, if you aren't too scared!

Part I:

History of Alcatraz

The Basic History of Alcatraz

From Spanish Exploration to Tourist Attraction....

One of the major factors that lead to the presence of ghosts in an area is the history of the location in which the spirits are ultimately found. A place with a long, rich history creates more fodder for spirits to have reason to linger. And a place with a turbulent, tragic history is conducive to the idea that there may be "unfinished business" for certain people, causing their disembodied souls to wander around trying to take care of the events in death that didn't work out for them in life. Because of this, understanding the history of an area is crucial to understanding the spirits who haunt the location.

Alcatraz is an island with a complex, detailed, and interesting history. Merely the setting of the place — situated in the rocky Bay waters in close proximity to the famous city of San Francisco — has made it a location with an interesting past. The details of that past reveal a series of tragic times. Life on the island had its ups and downs, and there are certainly those who had positive experiences there, but the location has seen more than its fair share of traumatic experiences. When such experiences are amassed by a number of people in such a small geographical location, negative energy is sure to build up, creating a vacuum of sorts in which spirits can easily become mired. To understand why ghosts haunt Alcatraz, you must delve into this history.

An Alcatraz Timeline[1]

1542: Spain makes claim to the land known as Alta California.

1769: Spanish explorers "discover" Alcatraz Island while miscalculating a voyage to Monterey.

1775: Juan Manuel de Ayala names the island "Isla de los Alcatraces" (Island of the Pelicans). Soldiers of U.S. Army later nickname it "The Rock."

1822: The Mexican Republic is granted independence, and with it, claim the small island.

1846: A private Mexican citizen receives a land grant for Alcatraz from the Mexican Republic with the condition that a navigation light is established on the island.

1848: The Mexican-American War ends; the United States claims control of California.

1848: The United States refuses to recognize any private ownership claims to Alcatraz. Since no lighthouse was built under the Mexican land grant, all claims are considered null and void. Alcatraz is deemed public land, property of the United States Government.

1849: The Gold Rush begins with the discovery of gold in the American River. San Francisco grows to a population of 35,000. The discovery of gold and population explosion creates an important need for a West Coast harbor defense.

1850: President Millard Fillmore earmarks Alcatraz and other land in and around the bay for harbor defenses.

1851: A Board of Engineers for the Pacific Coast is established to oversee construction of major harbor forts. Original estimate for construction of fortress on Alcatraz Island was a conservative $300,000 (actual cost through 1869 – $1,600,000).

1854: After two years of construction, first lighthouse on Alcatraz (and the West Coast) lit with whale oil. Prior to its completion, several vessels sank in the Bay.

1859: Company H of the Third U.S. Artillery, led by Captain Joseph Stewart, takes command of Alcatraz. Biggest guns on Alcatraz were 60,000-pound cast iron, fifteen-inch Rodmans with a three-mile range. At a high point 433 men were assigned to Alcatraz.

1861: The Civil War begins; Alcatraz military forces ordered on high alert. Any ship flying confederate flag ordered captured or sunk.

1863: The U.S. Navy foils elaborate plan by Confederate sympathizers aboard the schooner *J.M. Chapman* and imprisons crew on Alcatraz.

1865: The Civil War ends, President Lincoln assassinated, Alcatraz soldiers sent to San Francisco to help keep order.

1868: Plans begin for a complete redesign of Alcatraz reflecting the nationwide standardization of battery design.

1870–1876: With little more than initial excavation by prison laborers completed, Congress cuts

An Alcatraz Timeline[1]

off appropriations for building national fortifications. Role of Alcatraz shifts from harbor defense to military prison.

1895: Nineteen members of the Hopi tribe are imprisoned on Alcatraz.

1899: Following the Spanish-American War, the U.S. Military recognizes the need for a modern prison facility on the West Coast. Prison population on Alcatraz grows to 441, overcrowding current structures.

1906: An earthquake hits San Francisco, damaging the municipal prison and forcing the transfer of prisoners to Alcatraz.

1907: War Department determines Alcatraz obsolete as a harbor-defense fort and designates it a permanent prison to serve the entire United States Army west of the Rockies. It's renamed "Pacific Branch US Military Prison, Alcatraz Island."

1908: New 84-foot concrete lighthouse tower constructed.

1909: $250,000 approved for construction of the world's largest concrete cell house. Plan calls for six hundred one-man cells within a five hundred foot-long structure to be built by convict laborers.

1912: New prison facility is completed.

1915: Alcatraz renamed "Pacific Branch, United States Disciplinary Barracks." New name reflects an emphasis on rehabilitation as well as punishment.

1930: The Great Depression and surge in organized crime leads to a military budget review of disciplinary barracks and search for new maximum security prison to house the nation's most incorrigible prisoners.

1934: Alcatraz is acquired by the Department of Justice and transformed into a United States Penitentiary. Military abandons Alcatraz, leaving behind thirty-two hard case prisoners, who were to become the first penitentiary inmates.

1934: Al Capone, "Machine Gun" Kelly, and Robert "Birdman" Stroud arrive on Alcatraz **1938**: Al Capone transferred from Alcatraz due to illness.

1962: Elaborate escape attempt made by Frank Lee Morris, and Clarence and John Anglin.

1963: Alcatraz penitentiary closes.

1969: Large group of Native Americans land on Alcatraz and claim the island as Indian property.

1970: During the Indians' occupation, a fire destroys the Warden's house and officers' club and damages the historic lighthouse.

1971: Federal Marshals descend on Alcatraz and arrest final Native American occupants for destruction of U.S. property.

1972: Congress creates the Golden Gate National Recreation Area, which includes Alcatraz.

1973: Alcatraz Island opens to the public; over one million people visit the National Park each year.

This history begins with Native American settlers in the Bay Area and the experiences of the early Spanish settlers who came to explore the region in which Alcatraz is located. It continues with the history of the island as a military prison. And it explains in brief detail about the most famous era of Alcatraz's past: its years as a maximum-security federal penitentiary. It is during this point in the history of the island that most of the tragic tales took place. Most of the spirits said to haunt the island had their living experiences at this time. Following the closure of the federal prison at Alcatraz, the island was abandoned until it was taken over by a group of Native American social activists who lived there for nearly two years, adding their imprint to the already dramatic tale of what had come before them.

And of course, today, Alcatraz is a tourist attraction drawing in visitors from around the globe. These people are leaving their marks on the history of Alcatraz even as you read this. And the more time that passes, the more change there is on Alcatraz... change that stirs up activity on that island. As this activity is stirred, it becomes more likely that unsettled spirits from days past are going to demand the attention of those coming to the island. Learning about the history of Alcatraz will help you to understand why these spirits stayed on this eerie island...but what it can't prepare you for is how this knowledge will affect you on your own trip to Alcatraz.

The Early Days

Spanish explorers discovered the area in which Alcatraz is located as early as 1542 when they first laid claim to what they then called "Alta California." Alcatraz Island itself wasn't named until 1775 when an exploration was led by Juan Manuel de Ayala for the purpose of charting all of the newly discovered and unnamed lands along the San Francisco Bay and the Pacific Coast region. Ayala gave the Island the Spanish appellation "Isla de los Alcatraces" (Alcatraz History, 2007). The name translates to Island of the Pelicans. It sounds almost like a name for a beautiful, tropical vacation destination, but the island was anything but pretty. In fact, Ayala and his crew proceeded along the coast with no exploration of the island because it "was totally uninhabited, plagued by barren ground, little vegetation and surrounding water that churned with swift currents" (Taylor, 2006). The setting surrounding Alcatraz was one that was enough to deter even these brave foragers into the new world from further exploration of what might lie on its shores.

Described throughout history with words like "frightening," "menacing," and "ominous," it's a setting that's naturally ideal for spirit activity. And indeed, even at the time of early Spanish exploration, it was believed that something indescribable, otherworldly, and definitely scary was happening on that island that had been so pleasantly, and mistakenly, named after the birds of the bay. Of course, even before Alcatraz was "discovered" and named, the area was known by the Native Americans who lived in the region. And even back then, it was believed that the area was haunted. Historical reports indicate that the Native American people "considered it to be the dwelling place of evil spirits," a fact which caused them to avoid going to the island "entirely out of respect for its inherent 'bad medicine'" (Ullman, 2006).

Approximately fifty years after the island was named by Ayala and his crew, the Mexican Republic obtained its independence from Spain and the area surrounding Alcatraz became part of Mexico. In 1846, a land grant for Alcatraz was given to a private citizen of Mexico, under the condition that a lighthouse would be established on the island (Alcatraz History, 2007). However, two years later (before the lighthouse could be built), the Mexican-American War came to its bloody end and the United States took control of the Bay Area region, including what became known as Alcatraz Island. The rights of the Mexican landowner ceased without question; he was hardly the last person whose life would be forever altered because of the political decisions related to the control of Alcatraz.

A Timeline[2]

1848: California becomes U.S. property at the end of the Mexican-American War. Gold is discovered along the American River and the Gold Rush begins.

1850: A joint Army and Navy commission recommends a Triangle of Defense to guard the San Francisco Bay. President Fillmore signs an Executive Order reserving lands around San Francisco Bay, including Alcatraz, for "public purposes."

1854: The Alcatraz lighthouse begins service as the first lighthouse on the Pacific Coast.

1859: Captain Joseph Stewart and eighty-six men of Company H, Third U.S. Artillery take command of Alcatraz.

1861: Confederates attack Fort Sumter and the Civil War begins. Colonel Jonhston prepares San Francisco defenses, and then resigns to serve the Confederacy.

1863: *J.M. Chapman*, a Confederate privateer ship, is seized and its crew is arrested and imprisoned on Alcatraz. Captain William Winder authorizes Alcatraz to fire a blank shot at *HMS Sutlej*. Lower Prison, a temporary wooden structure, is built. Other prison structures are added on to it soon after.

1865: Alcatraz troops are sent to San Francisco to preserve peace and prevent rioting after President Lincoln's assassination. Alcatraz cannons fire the official mourning for the dead president.

1870: Major George Mendell designs plans for earthwork defenses on Alcatraz.

1876: The Centennial Great Sham Battle proves Alcatraz defenses are not adequate.

1895: Nineteen Hopis are imprisoned on Alcatraz.

1898: The Spanish-American War results in prison overcrowding at Alcatraz.

1900: The Upper Prison is built on the Parade Ground.

1907: Alcatraz is designated as the "Pacific Branch, U.S. Military Prison."

1912: The new cell house, built with convict labor, is completed and prisoners are moved in.

1915: Alcatraz is renamed the "United States, Disciplinary Barracks."

1933: Alcatraz is transferred to the Federal Bureau of Prisons. Thirty-two of the worst prisoners remain on the island in federal custody.

The History

Just one year after America gained control of California, the Gold Rush happened and the San Francisco Bay Area began to swell with new settlers. As a result, issues of national security came to the forefront of military concerns and it was quickly determined that Alcatraz would be best used by the military as a region for defense of the area (Alcatraz History, 2007). The island was perfectly situated with a view of San Francisco, giving the military a place where they could easily guard over the city. This decision was confirmed the following year, 1850, under the order of President Millard Fillmore. One year following that order, the government established a Board of Engineers for the Pacific Coast whose duty was to oversee the construction of major harbor forts in the area.

The development of Alcatraz as an area for national defense did not come cheaply. In 1851, the Board of Engineers of the Pacific Coast estimated that constructing a fortress on Alcatraz would cost the U.S. Government $300,000. The actual cost spent over the next eighteen years for development of Alcatraz was over $1.5 million. The late 1850s were spent developing the island with an eye towards maintaining military control over the region's natural gold resource. This development began with the construction of a lighthouse, which was completed in 1854. The lighthouse served partially as a watchtower to keep an eye out for impending descent on the area by foreign countries interested in the gold harbored along the West Coast. Although serving this practical purpose of protection of the area, the lighthouse also became an important tourist draw to the San Francisco Bay Area, due in no small part to the fact that it was the first operating lighthouse to be constructed anywhere along the Pacific Coast (Alcatraz History, 2007). This lighthouse would also be one of the first areas of Alcatraz to turn up in the history of hauntings on the island; though the original lighthouse is now gone, it sometimes can be seen on foggy nights in the spot where it was originally constructed. It fades in and out, often barely visibly in the fog, flashing its light at those who care to notice.

Of course, the lighthouse was important to the construction of Alcatraz, but it was only one part of the development of the military fortress at Alcatraz. Great attention was given to the development of the island and "after several years of laborious construction and various armament expansions, Alcatraz was established as the United States' western symbol of military strength" (Alcatraz History, 2007). The cost of this expansion was not only monetary—lives were also lost. "The first reported ones were in 1857 where Daniel Pewter and Jacob Unger passed away under a landslide while excavating between the wharf and the guard-house" (Alcatraz Hauntings, 2007). And so began the story of death on Alcatraz and perhaps the groundwork for how it came to be a place where people were likely to get stuck in the transition from life to death.

In 1859, the area of Alcatraz came under the control of Company H of the Third U.S. Artillery; over four hundred men were assigned to the location (Alcatraz History, 2007). Military activity in the area only grew when the Civil War began in 1961. The forces that were stationed on Alcatraz Island were placed on high alert and ordered to either capture or sink any ship that was seen flying a confederate flag. In 1863, a crew of Confederate sympathizers was captured by the U.S. Navy and imprisoned on Alcatraz Island. These were the first men whose freedom was taken at Alcatraz. They may have also been the first large group of desperate people to lose their lives — and their souls — to this location. Although this incarceration took place, the main role of Alcatraz at this time remained defense of the harbor, not use as a military prison.

It wasn't until the middle of the 1870s that the focus of Alcatraz shifted towards its eventual role as an island of incarceration. Up until that time, military troops were stationed on the island to maintain control of the area and development of the island was in line with the standards necessary to improve the area as a region for defense. However, maintenance of the military armaments on the island required money and time and it wasn't long before the island of Alcatraz wasn't serving well as a military fortress. In fact, "within a few decades the island's role as a military fortress would start to fade away, and its defenses would become obsolete by the standards of more modern weaponry" (Alcatraz History, 2007). Additionally, as the excited panic associated with the 1849 California Gold Rush died down, so did the need to rigidly protect the area from the perceived threat of foreign thieves In the mid 1870s, funds for the purpose of improving the armaments of the military ceased and the area began to be used primarily as a military prison. Growth of the prison continued throughout the end of the nineteenth century. However, it wasn't until 1907 that it was officially determined that Alcatraz would no longer be used for defense of the harbor. At that time it was renamed the Pacific Branch US Military Prison, Alcatraz Island (Alcatraz History, 2007).

This announcement didn't happen accidentally. It had been a long time in coming, but the final straw was the occurrence and effects of San Francisco's 1906 Earthquake. This critically important part of San Francisco's history did not leave Alcatraz unaffected. Although the earthquake's physical damage did not

A light still flashes today in the lighthouse of Alcatraz. The original lighthouse was the first working lighthouse on the Pacific Coast, drawing tourists to San Francisco in the early twentieth century.

extend to the island in the bay, the effects were clearly felt there as civilian prisoners contained within city limits were immediately moved to Alcatraz for safekeeping. The island's unique ability to hold the nation's criminals was noted, the official determination that the island would be a military prison was made, and additional construction began.

Development of the prison continued for the next several years, including construction of a new lighthouse as well as prison-labor construction of "the world's largest concrete cell house" (Alcatraz History, 2007). The largest part of the cell house, completed in 1912, can still be seen today on the central crest of Alcatraz Island (Alcatraz History, 2007). In 1915, Alcatraz was renamed once again, this time being called Pacific Branch, United States Disciplinary Barracks. This name change was a brief attempt to reflect changes in punishment styles towards a yen for rehabilitation although it was one that was more superficial than actual. By 1920, the prison was filled to capacity with army prisoners. It "was the army's first long-term prison, and it was already beginning to build its reputation as a tough detention facility by exposing inmates to harsh confinement conditions and ironhanded discipline" (Alcatraz History, 2007). The harshness of the conditions at Alcatraz would become the hallmark of the institution. And it was this harshness that deepened the desperation, violence, fear, and tragedy that would take place on the island in the years to come. This harshness would help solidify the foundation of Alcatraz as a place where souls could easily become stuck.

Right: The people of San Francisco didn't like the ugliness of the Alcatraz prison. Vegetation was planted to help beautify the grounds. Today, the grounds are maintained by the U.S. National Park Service.

It may have been commended as a harsh institution, but the days of the military prison as a punitive location were numbered. In spite of the fact that the prison was appreciated for being a tough place of punishment for those housed within its confines, the people of San Francisco were not pleased with the fact that this ugly location lay in the middle of their beautiful bay. "The public disliked having an Army prison as a sterile focal point in the middle of the beautiful San Francisco Bay, so the Military made arrangements to have soil from Angel Island brought over, and it was spread throughout the acreage of Alcatraz. Several prisoners were trained as able gardeners, and they planted numerous varieties of flowers and decorative plants to give the island a more pleasing appearance from the mainland" (Alcatraz History, 2007).

The people living in San Francisco and the tourists drawn to the area by its regional beauty may have been impressed with the attention given to the landscape at Alcatraz, but it added yet another cost to the upkeep of the already expensive island. In 1934, the military determined that the rising operational costs of the prison had begun to outweigh the benefits of keeping the prison in operation and so closed down the institution (Alcatraz History, 2007). Responsibility for, and control of, the prison at Alcatraz reverted to the Department of Justice and thus began the period of island prison life, which ultimately made Alcatraz infamous.

Federal Prison at Alcatraz

A Partial Timeline

1934: The federal prison at Alcatraz is opened. The first warden is James A. Johnston. The first prisoners are thirty-two military prisoners who were incarcerated in the military prison on Alcatraz. Shortly afterwards, the first civilian prisoners arrived. These included famous names like Al Capone and George "Machine Gun" Kelly.

1935: Inmate Rufe McCain arrives at the prison as a transfer from Leavenworth. *(Leavenworth, a maximum-security prison in Kansas, was one of the toughest prisons in the country before Alcatraz become a federal prison.)* Henri Young also arrives at Alcatraz during this time.

1938: An escape attempt by several inmates ends in the death of one of the prison guards. Also during this year, Roy Gardner is released from his four-year-stint at Alcatraz; he writes his autobiography called *Hellcatraz*.

1940: Henri Young fatally stabs Rufe McCain. It is said that one or both of these men haunts McCain's old cell. Outside of the prison, Roy Gardner commits suicide in his motel room.

1942: Robert "Birdman" Stroud arrives at the prison as a transfer from Leavenworth. A death sentence has been commuted and he is sentenced to live in solitary confinement for the rest of his life.

1946: One of the bloodiest escape attempts ever takes place. It is led by inmates Coy, Cretzer, and Hubbard. They take over the prison for several days, killing two guards. The military is called in to regain control of the prison; the escapees are killed in the takeover.

1962: Frank Lee Morris and the Anglin brothers escape from Alcatraz. It is believed that they died in the water surrounding the prison, but the facts are never determined.

1963: The federal prison at Alcatraz closes its doors.

An Incarceration Island

The eyes of the government turned towards making Alcatraz a federal prison during the early 1930s. To understand the early days of the development of Alcatraz as a federal prison, one has to have an understanding of the time period during which the prison was initially in operation. This was during The Great Depression and fear was prevalent all over America. In the mid 1930s, social issues were creating large pockets of crime. Prohibition was in action, the Depression was causing problems for everyone and what emerged out of this was a thriving illegal underground that was run by the gangsters frequently depicted in modern-day movies about the era. The government faced a two-fold problem; it needed to find something to do with the major criminals who were already wreaking havoc in the nation and it needed to find a way to limit the reach and spread of new big crime bosses. "Alcatraz was the ideal solution to the problem. It could serve the dual purpose of incarcerating public enemies while standing as a visible icon, a warning to this new and ruthless brand of criminal" (Alcatraz History, 2007).

In 1934, control of Alcatraz was transferred from the United States Military to the United States Department of Justice. The first thing the federal government saw fit to do was re-vamp the image of the prison to make it seem more menacing. This was hardly difficult to do since the mere sight of Alcatraz sitting in the bay has been frightening to people in the area for hundreds of years. The federal government deconstructed all of the work that had been done previously by the gardeners of the military prison

Left: This is the key to the gun gallery that overlooks the inmates' cells. The keys were sent up to the gallery for safekeeping during the shifts of the guards.

Changes made to the prison included:

• Cementing over the old utility tunnels to eradicate the ability of a prisoner to enter and then hide in them.

• Construction of multiple guard towers across the island. As described by author Jolene Babyak, "One tower was a coal black, octagonal cell with shatterproof glass. Three stories tall, it sat atop four spider legs and a spiral staircase, which ended at a locked hatch in the deck. Of the six towers it was the principal post, located on the dock and staffed twenty-four hours a day." There was also the Road (or Two Tower), Main Tower, Power House Tower, the Hill tower and the Model Roof tower. The latter three "were manned only during daylight hours and mostly protected the Industries area when convicts were out of their cells."

• Design of special gun galleries that were installed above the reach of prisoners so that armed guards could watch over the inmates below them from behind iron rod barriers.

• Installation of newly developed metal detectors in the dining hall and other strategic locations throughout the island.

• Installation of tool-proof window coverings on all areas that would be accessible to the future inmates of the new federal prison.

• Permanent installation of tear-gas canisters in the dining hall that could be remotely activated by guards from multiple points within the prison.

• Replacement of the soft, square bars of the cells with tool-proof hardened bars of the most modern variety (Alcatraz History, 2007).

to soften the appearance of the island for the people of San Francisco. Then the federal government renovated the existing structure to alter the attitude emanated by Alcatraz. Under the direction of Robert Burge (one of the nation's foremost security experts at the time), the prison was reconstructed to be both outwardly foreboding and reportedly escape-proof (Alcatraz History, 2007).

"The implementation of these new measures, combined with the natural isolating barriers created by the icy Bay waters, meant that the prison was ready to receive the nation's most incorrigible criminals" (Alcatraz History, 2007). When the military left the island, they left behind thirty-two of "the worst of the worst" inmates. These were the first prisoners of the federal penitentiary. Others quickly followed. "In August, 1934, a group of fifty-three inmates was taken from Atlanta Federal Prison, chained hand foot, and loaded onto a train headed for California. The train had special steel coaches with barred windows and wire mesh doors, because its cargo consisted of the most wanted criminals in the history of the United States penal system. One was Al Capone" (Heaney, 1987, p. 24).

Indeed, big names like Capone were the first prisoners to arrive at Alcatraz. These are names that are still recognized today, and the spirits attached to these names are said to remain at the prison. For almost thirty years, these men—and other criminals like them—lived out isolated lives on the island of Alcatraz. The horrors that happened behind those walls were unspeakable...and the tragedies that took place there amongst those violent criminals left scars that remain to this day. Perhaps it is in the nature of storytelling for the ghosts of Alcatraz to be reported to be those infamous folks who helped glorify the prison during their lifetimes. Perhaps there is little truth to the ghost stories surrounding their pasts, but whether or not the sightings are accurate, the lasting impression these guys left on the people visiting Alcatraz is undeniable.

Life on Alcatraz was filled with the kind of desperation that only comes from the unnatural condition of placing a large number of extraordinarily violent offenders together in a setting controlled almost entirely by domination and fear. Alcatraz "was a place of total punishment and minimum privilege. And those who survived it often did so at the cost of their sanity...and some believe their souls" (Taylor, 2006).

Although regular imprisonment on Alcatraz was bad, there were places within the prison that were even worse than the normal cells for many of the prisoners. The solitary confinement cells (known as "the hole" by most inmates) were places of total sensory deprivation and isolation. These cells were lonely, dark, and frightening—an environment conducive to fear and a setting that is believed to have trapped spirits. In the early days of the federal prison, there were also dungeon cells located near A-Block. These cells, where prisoners were locked to the wall with a ball and chain, were rapidly determined to violate the eighth amendment against cruel and unusual punishment and so their use was discontinued. But during the time that they were in use, they trapped the men — and perhaps their souls — in a place that was dark, damp, and appropriately known as a dungeon.

As a federal prison with extreme punitive measures in place, Alcatraz was nationally recognized, but it was a prison that was only in operation for a scant thirty years. As the military had before it, the federal government eventually found that the upkeep of the prison was just too costly. Combined with negative news attention resulting from the several failed escape attempts and the one arguable successful escape, which took place towards the end of the prisons' life, there was less and less reason to keep funneling funds into Alcatraz. The prison closed its doors in 1963. "The island remained essentially abandoned while several parties lobbied the government with ideas for development, ranging from a West Coast version of the Statue of Liberty to a shopping center/hotel complex" (Alcatraz History, 2007).

The prisoners that were still left on the island at the time of its closing were moved to other prisons around the country. But it is believed that some of them could never escape the things that happened to them while they were isolated on Alcatraz and people report that their spirits have returned to the island to haunt this portion of their past. Some of the prisoners who haunt Alcatraz are the infamous names that terrified — and fascinated — the American public with their lives of crime. Others are merely common violent criminals with little-remembered stories and less-remembered names. But they are all equally frightening when they turn up on the island today, unable to leave behind the horrors of their lives and so stay to haunt the prison and the people who visit it.

Native American Occupation

The federal prison at Alcatraz closed down at a time when political tensions in the country were high. Social activism was beginning to take root on many levels. Prisons were being encouraged to enter into new models focusing on rehabilitation instead of punishment. Social inequities in incarceration related to race and economic status were starting to gain exposure. And general awareness of all types of social imbalance and inequity was the topic of the day, especially in liberal San Francisco. Native American activism was one portion of this part of the history of the United States—and Alcatraz played a large role in this activism, both locally and throughout the nation.

In 1964, the year after the federal prison was shut down, a group of Sioux Indians landed on Alcatraz, claiming rights to it under the Fort Laramie 1868 Sioux Treaty (Public Broadcasting Service, 2002). The treaty allowed "non-reservation Indians to claim land the government had taken for forts and other uses and had later abandoned" (Eagle, 1992, p. 14). The goal of the takeover was to gain attention in the area for the plight of the Bay Area's Native American people. Their intention was "to test the validity of the 1868 treaty and remind people of the more than six hundred treaties which had been broken and other injustices which were still being committed against Native Americans by the federal government" (Eagle, 1992, p. 15).

Another issue they were raising awareness about was a recent unjust monetary offer made by the federal government to the Native American people for the land that was taken over during the Gold Rush. In an attempt to resolve the problems of the past, the government was offering forty-seven cents per acre for the land that had been illegally taken. The Sioux takeover of Alcatraz pointed out that the Indian people would be happy to pay the government that going rate of forty-seven cents per acre, making the total they owed for the island less than ten dollars (Eagle, 1992, 16).

During the brief few hours that they were on the island, the Native American people staked their claim to various parts of the land there. They officially wrote down their claims and prepared them to be sent to the Bureau of Land Management in Sacramento. However, it wasn't long before they were asked to leave the island. Just about two hours after their arrival, they were met by the acting warden, Richard J. Willard, who demanded that they leave the island or be arrested for trespassing. The issue was discussed and it was determined that the Native American people did not want their actions to be seen as "police-baiting," so they agreed to leave peacefully (Eagle, 1992, p. 17). They remained for only four hours, but their imprint on the island was far from short-lived (Public Broadcasting Service, 2002).

"The event was publicized and remembered, and it also made some of (the Indian people) wonder whether that gloomy and crumbling fortress might one day be turned into a resource for Indian people. After the brief Sioux invasion, (they) kept thinking about Alcatraz, and the ball began rolling in the direction of the much bigger and longer-lasting Indian occupation of 1969" (Eagle, 1992, p. 18). Also, events in the Native American community in the area continued to unfold, giving them more reasons to keep thinking about the possibilities of Alcatraz.

As part of the activism of the era, numerous tribal groups were setting aside their personal differences and coming together. The United Council was formed in the early 1960s and was gaining members and power in the area. After the 1964 invasion of Alcatraz, the group began discussing the possibilities for pursuing legal action. They made plans to petition the United States government for the land under the original treaty, but the plans never materialized. Then...there were two major events that ultimately led to the 1969 occupation of Alcatraz (Eagle, 1992, p. 36–38).

First, there was discussion of a Texas billionaire purchasing the land from the federal government (Eagle, 1992, p. 39). This would mean that the treaty would no longer apply. Shortly following this announcement, there was an event that was of more importance to the Native American community. The date was October 10, 1969. The event was the burning down of the San Francisco Indian Center on Valencia Street (Eagle, 1992, p. 40). The location had served the social needs of over 30,000 Native American locals. The need for a new center re-focused Native American attention on claiming Alcatraz as Indian land (Public Broadcasting Service, 2002).

In 1969, six years after Alcatraz ceased to be a federal prison, it was claimed by a Native American activist group who believed that they had rights to the island

as Native American property (Alcatraz History, 2007).
It took two attempts to make the takeover happen. The
first happened in two parts on November 9. During the
daytime, a group gathered for the eyes of the media with
the intention of landing on Alcatraz. Problems with the
boat made it impossible to get all the way to Alcatraz,
although the boat got close enough to the island that
several Native Americans jumped into the water and
tried to swim there. One, Joe Bill, made it. The group
returned to San Francisco and tinkered with their plans.
That night, with no media fanfare, a smaller group went
out to the island. Fourteen of them landed on Alcatraz
in that first takeover.

In the morning, the Indian occupation was announced
to the media. This resulted in an extensive search of the
island. The Native American people hid out in various
locations all throughout Alcatraz, letting the officials
continue to search for them. When the search had gone
on for hours, they peacefully revealed themselves. They
read their proclamation and explained what their plans

When Native American activists took over Alcatraz Island, they declared all Indians welcome at the former prison.

were. They announced that the occupation marked the establishment of their squatters' rights on the island and stated their intention to return. Then they "evacuated the island voluntarily in the hope that something could be worked out in accordance with the objectives of the Proclamation" (Eagle, 1992, p. 69–70). Later that month, nearly one hundred American Indians (primarily, but not entirely, college students), took control of the island (Public Broadcasting Service, 2002). The group called themselves Indians of All Tribes to reflect the fact that a number of different groups had come together in this movement (Eagle, 1992, p. 44).

Why did the Native American people takeover Alcatraz? Well, for one thing, they needed a place to assemble since their building had been burned down. Alcatraz was the right choice for a number of reasons, not the least of which was that it was originally Native American land that had been taken over by the American government. In their initial proclamation, Indians of All Tribes explained that they would gladly pay back the government the going rate (the aforementioned forty-seven cents per acre). They also sarcastically pointed out that the government should be happy for Alcatraz to be used as Native American land since it so closely resembled the reservations of the modern day. Similarities they pointed out included its lack of running water, transportation, health care, and adequate education facilities (Eagle, 1992, p. 45).

But the Native American people intended for this occupation to be more than just a sort of awareness raising. It was also meant to serve the purpose of setting up the facilities so needed by the Indian community. They planned to erect a Center for Native American Studies, an American Indian Spiritual Center, an Indian Center of Ecology, A Great Indian Training School, and an American Indian Museum (Eagle, 1992, p. 46– 47). Some of these goals would be met during the following year and a half when the island remained under the control of the Native American people.

Most people who came to the island stayed there for only a short time — a few days, a couple of weeks — but there was consistently a relatively large group of Native Americans on Alcatraz during the occupation. This was because of the effort that the Native American people had put into spreading the word about their actions. They drew media attention to their cause and they enlisted the assistance of the national Indian community. Major leaders in the social movements of the time paid attention to what was happening here. And word spread that continued support of this group could encourage social change.

"Visitors streamed into Alcatraz almost constantly, especially in the early days. For many Indians, the trip to Alcatraz became almost a pilgrimage. After all, it was the only piece of land in the country "owned" by Indians of All Tribes, which meant that every Indian owned a piece of "the Rock." And Indians were welcome on Alcatraz. If they chose to stay, after a week they were considered a resident and could participate in the governing of the island. This new Indian community attracted all kinds of Indians: college students, reservation Indians, "street people," mainland working people (Eagle, 1992, p. 91).

It was certainly an exciting time, and many of the initial goals of the Proclamation, such as the opening of an Indian school, came to fruition. But all was not well on the island. There were power struggles between the people living on Alcatraz and their Indian counterparts back on the mainland. And there were power struggles among different tribal groups on the island. Drugs and alcohol fueled these problems despite the leadership's best attempts to keep these items off of the island. So, although life there was exciting, it was also dramatic. (Eagle, 1992, p. 111–115)

And the problems weren't just amongst the Native American people, but also between them and the federal government. In light of the explosive political nature of the times, the government was slow and methodical in its treatment of the situation. Initially, they attempted to block supplies from coming to the island, but this plan was called off after three days because of the sheer number of boats that ran the blockades. Then they proceeded to spend a month in negotiations with the group, offering alternatives to no avail. Finally, in May of 1970, they began to crack down. This started with removing the water barge that supplied fresh water to Alcatraz. They also withdrew their own caretakers from the island and then cut off all electricity. (Eagle, 1992, p. 121–124)

The Native Americans refused to succumb to the pressure. But, in June of 1970, two devastating fires simultaneously broke out on the island. They destroyed the Warden's house and the officers' club and did damage to the historic lighthouse (Alcatraz History, 2007). To this day, the cause of the fire is unknown. At the time, the government claimed that the Indians had purposely set the fires and the Indians claimed that the government had sent in saboteurs to cause the blaze (Eagle, 1992, p. 127).

Despite these problems, the federal government maintained its slow approach to dealing with the "problem" at Alcatraz. The Native American people continued occupation of the island for another year. On June 11, 1971, the federal government had their chance to take the island back and they did so. A large group of the occupants had traveled to the city for the day to visit with family and take care of mainland chores. This left only fifteen Indians on the island that day. (Eagle, 1992, p. 132–133) Federal marshals moved in under orders to regain control of Alcatraz Island. The Native American activists who still remained there were arrested and charged with destruction of United States Property (Alcatraz History, 2007). There was no blood shed in the takeover, but tears stuck to the soil as the Native American people were led away from the island. Some say that you can still hear their cries of surrender whipping through the wind.

And reportedly, there was one little girl who got left behind. It should be noted that there were no child deaths reported at Alcatraz during this time. (However, the teenage daughter of Richard Oakes, one of the most well-known activists, did sustain fatal injuries at the island. She fell down a flight of stairs in the officers' quarters and was injured. She was taken to a hospital in the city, but she died there of the injuries. (Eagle, 1992, p. 110) Perhaps a young peer of hers recalls this tragedy, because it is said that there is a little girl whose spirit remains on the island, haunting what used to be the mortuary for the federal prisoners who died there. Maybe her unique childhood on the island during this period of activism gave her an intense empathy for the social inequity that brought these men to live and die in incarceration and so she cries for them there. Or maybe her own (good and bad) experiences on Alcatraz led her to become stuck there, returning upon her death to continue the awareness-raising she had been a part of in her youth. After all, the years of Native American occupation of Alcatraz had many joys, but they also had their struggles and they ultimately ended in surrender.

Alcatraz Today

In 1972, Congress created the Golden Gate National Recreation Area, which includes Alcatraz Island. The following year, Alcatraz Island was opened to the public as a tourist attraction. Today, over one million people annually visit the Island (Alcatraz History, 2007). These tourists fill Alcatraz with their sounds of laughter and life, but their jubilance can't erase the horrible history that happened on that small space of land jutting out from the bay.

"During the day, the old prison is a bustling place, filled with tour guides and visitors...but at night, the building is filled with the inexplicable. Many believe that the energy of those who came to serve time on the Rock still remains, that Alcatraz is an immense haunted house...a place where strange things can and do happen today!" (Taylor, 2006)

And so, when you book your tickets to experience Alcatraz for yourself, remember that it's going to be more than just your typical tourist experience. When you stand on the edge of San Francisco, waiting to get onto the ferry that will take you just over one mile out into the Bay, you will likely have to wrap your arms tightly around yourself to ward away the chill. Sure, it's partially the chill from the wind that continuously whips through the area. And it's also the chill that is felt because of the mist from the fog that permeates the Bay. But there's something about the chill that goes beneath your skin. It is more than the chill of the weather...it is the chill of the past.

Part II

The Setting

Traveling to Alcatraz

From the Ferry Dock to the Cell House Tour

In order to understand the history and hauntings of Alcatraz Island, you really need to get a good sense of what it is like to spend time on the island. You have to be able to hear the whistling of the wind through the empty cells, to feel the fear of being entirely enshrouded in fog, to sense the terrifying isolation of being so close to active life and yet so far away from anyone who loves you. This chapter will help you to get a sense of what it is like to stand on Alcatraz today and to understand the numerous reasons that this place is so conducive to spirit activity and sightings of unusual events.

If you have never been to Alcatraz, this chapter will transport you there, helping you to get a good feel for the setting of the island. And if you've already stepped foot on Alcatraz in your past, reading this will remind you of what it was like to be on that island and why you were probably ready to leave when your trip was over. And it will explain why the small little space that makes up Alcatraz Island is so rich with spirits who are not able to leave the area though they probably desperately want to find the light and move on.

The island IS undeniably spooky....

Following the description of what it is like to be on Alcatraz today, you will find a map depicting all of the areas on the island that are said to be haunted. As you will see, there is hardly a spot on Alcatraz that hasn't had some history of ghost activity. Brief descriptions of the haunted areas follow, but the real stories will be found in the later pages of the book. Do you dare to proceed?

The View of Alcatraz

When you book tickets to visit Alcatraz Island as a tourist today, you wait with a large crowd of people at the dock of the boat, preparing to take the short trip over to the island. Children are running around excitedly, young couples from foreign countries are standing with their arms around each other in shelter from the windy chill, and travelers of all ages are eagerly awaiting their educational and entertaining experience on the island. On a good day, as you stand to wait for your ferry ride, you will be able to see Alcatraz clearly. On a bad day, the fog will be so thick that you'll have trouble even locating its spot in the bay despite the fact that it lies just over a mile away from where you stand. All you'll be able to make out is the dim light from the lighthouse coming through the clouds … and if you know that a phantom lighthouse sometimes appears, you'll probably wonder if even this vision is one really being seen by your straining eyes.

Sitting within the beauty of the San Francisco Bay is Alcatraz, a prison emanating the desolation that once filled its walls.

In his memoir about his experiences as a prison guard at Alcatraz, George H. Gregory describes the moments before he made his first boat trip to the island, when he was standing in the city awaiting whatever fate might be in store for him. He writes, "I stood for a minute looking out at "The Rock." Which was just barely visible in the fog. For the first time, I felt a grim chill — a feeling that I would experience regularly throughout my tenure on Alcatraz" (Gregory, 2002, p. 13). You don't have to be a prison guard heading to duty to feel this sense of imminent doom. The "grim chill" is something that the island of Alcatraz emanates out towards everyone. On a foggy day, you can't even see anything on Alcatraz except for the lighthouse...which looms eerily amidst the clouds. And yet, whether you see the buildings of Alcatraz or not, you can feel the chill it sends in your direction.

And it is almost impossible to imagine how threatening the island can appear at night. In his book about the Native American occupation of Alcatraz, Adam Fortune Eagle describes what the island looked like as the boat pulled up during the night. "The underwater cable warning sign glowed with a ghostly bluish light and the mournful moan of the island's two foghorns grew louder as we approached the island. It was hard to decide if the foghorns were there to drive off evil spirits or if Alcatraz itself was the spirit — an evil spirit with a circling Cyclopes eye and an awful voice sweeping across the waters" (Eagle, 1992, p. 62).

Yes, Alcatraz at night IS a scary thing indeed....

But let's imagine that it is a good day and that you can see Alcatraz as you wait for your ride. The skies are clear and the beauty of the bay captures your attention. To the far left of the island, you see the famous Golden Gate Bridge that arches across the water in all of its red-orange glory and rich history. Closer to Alcatraz, you see the hulking shape of Angel Island where hikers and picnickers enjoy the nature of the Bay Area and the varied history that is held there. To the right of Alcatraz, you see the modern architecture of the buildings in the East Bay and perhaps even a portion of the striking Bay Bridge. And in the middle of all of this beauty, in your direct line of sight, sits Alcatraz.

On a bad weather day, this island is but a menacing blip in a darkening bay. But on a good day, when the rest of the bay is beautiful, the contrasting ugliness of Alcatraz can seem even more threatening than it does on a bad day. Jolene Babyak, the daughter of a prison guard who grew up on the island, describes the memory of such a sight. She writes, "Alcatraz was perhaps the most beautiful home I've ever had. On a breezy, crystal-clear day, the bay is a magical setting, with two bridges — one, the Golden Gate, perhaps the most famous bridge in the world — defining the perimeters of the dramatic skyline of San Francisco. The bay itself was breathtaking theatre. Ships slid under the Golden Gate past our island; plugged-nosed tug boats churned up the white caps. The waves were frequently dotted with boats and their glistening white, yawning sails. Yet, there stood Alcatraz, a mile-and-a-quarter out in the bay, a battleship-shaped rock mounted with a three-story institutional-yellow prison. A flat island mountain lined with barbed wire and guard towers" (Babyak, 1988, p. 4).

Imposing isn't the right word to describe this island. It is too small to be imposing. Its faded colors are too drab to be menacing. But there is something about viewing the island that leaves you unsettled even on these clearest of days. You can't see the fencing. You know that there aren't prisoners living out violent, fear-filled lives there anymore. But it is almost as if the sadness and pain and desperation that mark the area's history hangs like an invisible cloud over the island, emanating negative energy back to the city. And as you look at the island that you are about to go visit, excited about the experience though you may be, a chill runs down your spine.

There IS something haunting this area....

Do You REALLY Want Off The Boat?

Arms wrapped around yourself to ward off the chill from the San Francisco wind and the sense of spirit activity you already feel inside your body, you wait in line to secure your place on the ferry over to Alcatraz. The gates open and your ticket is taken so you walk down what feels like a gangplank to board the boat. The boat is large and comfortable, designed for tourists, with a bar and snacks in the bottom deck and a large seating area up top. Despite its size and comfortable design, the boat still feels shaky as it wobbles in the wave of the bay. You consider getting a drink from the bar to quell your nerves, but you get the feeling that you might need all of your faculties as you explore this desperate island.

You make your way to the top of the boat and find a seat there so you can see whatever there is to see. Perhaps you even stand at the edge of the boat, looking out into the bay as you wait for everyone to get settled and for

A view of the city of San Francisco as the ferry to Alcatraz pulls away from the dock.

A view of Alcatraz from the ferry as it approaches the island.

the ride to begin. The boat takes off and immediately you can feel the temperature dropping. The wind whips around you, causing the hood on your jacket to flutter and the chill in the air to go straight to your bones. The fog circles around the boat, and the further that you get from the city, the harder it is to make out the distinct lines of the buildings that you are leaving behind.

As the city fades and you are no longer able to distract yourself with its picturesque beauty, you turn your attention to the boat, looking around at the people who are riding to Alcatraz with you. The children who are visiting the island with their parents, getting a little bit of historical education along with their trip to this fabulous city. The foreign twenty-somethings who are traveling the globe and just want to learn more about this strange part of the Bay Area's past. The locals who are showing off the area to their house guests and, perhaps, visiting this small island for the very first time since it's a spot that they often assume is best left to visitors. If something horrible happens and you get stuck on the island, these are the people who are going to be your companions. Your eyes move across this group and something that you can't quite see manages to somehow catch your eye. Is that a human shadow over in the corner of the noisy boat? You shake your head and shrug it away.

As you look around at the ethereal fog and see the water whipping up beneath the boat, you can't help but imagine what this ride must have been like for the prisoners who were transported to the island years ago. You don't know much about their stories yet, but you can envision the finality of that ride. The prisoners who were sent to spend time on Alcatraz when it was a maximum-security federal penitentiary were considered the "worst of the worst" and there was no way that most of them expected to leave the prison alive. You can practically feel the shackles of the past grip your ankles and you are almost overwhelmed by the inexplicable but insistent feeling that perhaps you should dive overboard.

This is what Alcatraz does to you. No matter how stable you are or how much you love your life, no matter how sure you are that you are just visiting the island to see one of the area's biggest attractions before getting a clam chowder bread bowl at a well-heated restaurant overlooking the Bay, Alcatraz gets into your soul and implants that sense of dread there within your heart. So many sad tales took place on that island, so often there was no one around (or no one who cared) to hear the cries of those who lost their lives (or at the very least, their spirits) during their brief stay there. So perhaps those spirits remain, calling out to the travelers who are trying to get to the island. Perhaps that is why you feel this sense of doom that you can't otherwise explain.

As your ferry reaches the island, pulling up close to the dock to let you and all of your companions off for the adventure of your San Francisco stay, you try to shake the invisible shackles from your legs. You look back at San Francisco. If you can see it at all through the seemingly omnipresent fog, the city seems unimaginably small. It's right there...and yet it is so far away. It's just a boat ride for you, but if there were no boat available, how would you get back to the city? The iciness of the waters prevents swimming, even if you had the stamina to make it that far. There would be *NO* escape.

As you exit the ferry that has brought you to this island of imprisonment, you glance back at it with longing, wondering just what you have gotten yourself into. From the corner of your eye, you think you see that shadow slip off the boat and enter the island. You can't pinpoint where it went. Your mind is probably just playing tricks on you. But what if it isn't?

Exploring Alcatraz Island

When you step off of the ferryboat, you have some options about where you are going. Unlike the prisoners who were transported here in chains (and even the prison guards and their families who once lived, worked, and played on the island), your freedom to explore is relatively unrestricted. Sure, there are forbidden areas that you are warned away from *"for your own safety,"* but you have some choices amongst the parts of Alcatraz that are open to the public.

Perhaps you start with the small group that has gathered around the speaker who is sharing a brief history of the island. Maybe you wander around the perimeter of the island, heading ever upwards, to see the way that the well-tended vegetation attempts to beautify the dilapidated buildings that stand here. Or maybe you make your way immediately to the guided audio tour that will tell you about the criminals who once lived — and died — in the cells that you are about to explore.

No matter which starting point you choose, one of the first things you notice, because it is simply impossible not to notice it, is the sound of birds all around you. They screech. They shriek. They sound almost like humans screaming, but they clearly are not human. If it is summer time, which is nesting season for the area's seagulls, you will find that the island is practically overrun by these birds. No matter how many tourists trek to Alcatraz, there seems to be more birds than people here during these months. And the language that they carry on amongst themselves seems to be filled with stories about activities that the travelers could never understand. What do these birds know about the secrets of this island? What is it that their animal instincts can sense in the air here? And why do they cry so loudly?

If you stand amidst the other travelers and close your eyes, you can clearly hear the cries of these birds.

Birds at Alcatraz shriek constantly, creating an eerie screaming that permeates the air.

And if you manage to find a quiet part of the island, off the beaten path where most of the other travelers are already exploring the human history of the prison, you may notice something in the pauses between their cries. What you notice is that there are sounds in between the distinct calls of the birds...sounds that don't really sound the same as the birds do, although they don't quite sound human either...Sounds that could very well be the cries of the island's ghosts. But you can't be sure.

It's enough to give anyone chills and you'll probably find that you quickly want to return to the group. The thing about Alcatraz is that the sounds here may be scary, but the silence is absolutely terrifying. The wardens of Alcatraz knew this. In fact, "in the beginning, there was the dreaded 'silent system,' a throwback to an era when prisoners were forbidden to converse. The silence would be deafening. And cruel. And increasingly difficult to enforce. Within four years, the rule was abandoned and never again brought back" (Babyak, 1988, p. 12).

When you catch the sounds of breaths and words amidst the cries of the birds on Alcatraz today, you are glad that this island is anything but silent now. You begin

A mother bird and her two growing babies at Alcatraz.

During the summertime, the birds that live in the San Francisco Bay Area come to Alcatraz to lay their eggs. These are a group of birds nesting on the island.

ALCATRAZ

AND THE

AMERICAN

PRISON EXPERIENCE

your journey so that you can drown out any remaining quiet eeriness. You start your trek in the exhibits at the bottom of the island. A theater is playing a short bilingual video about the history of Alcatraz, and perhaps you get a coffee from the store there so that you can try to warm up while you learn about the island. But the coffee can do nothing to erase the chill.

Alcatraz IS a COLD, COLD place....

The exhibits are set in rooms off of a hallway that reeks of terror. You step out of the theater to face these rooms and to your left can see this hallway, at the end of which is emptiness. Nothing lies there, and yet, you can sense movement in the air here. You enter the furthest of the rooms and see an exhibit depicting information about the oldest prisoners of Alcatraz.

Opposite: A series of exhibits about Alcatraz is located in rooms just off of this main hallway. Despite the number of tourists at the island, this area is often deserted.

Walking further down the hallway, there is nothing but a vast stretch of emptiness.

These are the prisoners that spent their sixties, seventies, and even eighties within the walls of Alcatraz. Their voices come out towards you from speakers that share their stories. Their bodies are long gone, but have their spirits left the building as well? Why do they keep these rooms so cold?

Moving on, you make your way to an exhibit about the history of the Native American people who took over the island for two years after the prison had closed down. Their faces beam out at you from framed pictures, the anguish and the joy of their Alcatraz experience carved into the lines on their faces. The ancient Native Americans once believed that Alcatraz was a place filled with evil spirits; the individuals in these pictures claimed the land and made it their own. But what happened to their souls when the federal government moved in and took the land back from them? Where are these people now? The video sharing their stories with you continues looping, but if it paused for even a moment, you might find that the whispering tales being shared are still there in the echoes of the empty room.

Exiting the hallway where these exhibits are held, you see a staircase. It is blocked off and seems to lead to nowhere.

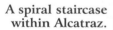

A spiral staircase within Alcatraz.

A set of stairs with NO destination....

You can't help but feel compelled to move as close to them as you can—to see the nothingness into which they lead and hope to find some answers there, answers that can explain away the uncomfortable feeling that arises within you from seeing a set of stairs heading up into emptiness. You want to see that they do indeed lead somewhere, that this isn't just a dead end on a dead island. You gaze upwards and eye the stairs, but all that's confirmed is that they lead to no place. Your unspoken questions go unanswered and your fear is not abated. And that's when you're certain that you hear it...a set of shackles dragging a ball down the staircase. But of course, you continue to look and see that no one is there. You turn away, sure that you are imagining things, but you can't shake the feeling that something—or someone—is following you down the hall. You maintain your self control because you don't want anyone else there to see you running away from what you're sure is nothing...but you pick up the pace a little bit because those shackles sound like they're closing in.

Exiting the exhibits, you can hear the bustle and laughter of the other tourists. Sound carries easily here and there are always plenty of people to keep the place occupied. You follow the group up the long winding pathway, which takes you up to the prison building and the location of your cell house audio tour. The sensation of the ghosts around you fades as you file into line to accept your audio equipment. The feelings from the past get lost amidst the fanny packs and electronic devices that frame your immediate view. But as you slip the earphones over your head, your thoughts become focused on the tales that you are about to hear. The sounds around you become muffled and you drift straight into your own experience of Alcatraz.

The audio tour allows you to take your time, pausing the tale, rewinding, and revisiting the past at your leisure. It takes you on a path through the cell house, where you learn the stories of the famous prisoners who were once housed here. You are not told about the ghosts of Alcatraz, but some of the names that you hear and the cells that you visit were once home to the people who are now said to haunt the island. You visit D Block, where the isolation rooms were once located. Following the instructions on the audio tour, you step inside the cellblocks. Trying to imagine living in a room that barely spans the length of your arm, without lighting and sometimes without heat, that increasingly familiar (but nevertheless infinitely uncomfortable) chill inevitably runs through your body.

You let the group wander ahead. You turn off your earphones and stand quietly in the cell. Maybe you are in D14, where the glowing eyes of a ghostly monster were said to haunt inmate Rufe McCain who later became a ghost here himself. Perhaps you have heard this famous story already and were too frightened to enter that haunted cell, so you stand instead inside of D11 or D12. You turn in a circle and eye the small room. As you exit through the cell doors, you may feel what many before you have reported feeling here: unsettling emotions and icy fingers touching the back of your neck.

You can't imagine what it would be like to be housed in these cells. You look back into them and wonder. What would it be like to hear those cell doors slam behind you? As described by Babyak in her account of life on the island, "Gears were located on either side of the cell block and could be maneuvered to close one or all cell fronts. The levers resembled ones used on the famed San Francisco cable cars. And in some ways, the sound of a closing cell door is like the sound of a cable car on tracks. But such pleasantries don't remain. What occurs is a drum roll of heavy metal thundering across metal and concrete, as the door slides into position with a final metal-to-metal collision that echoes throughout the concrete

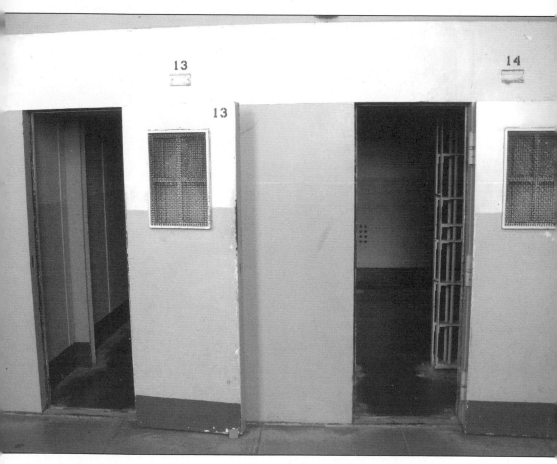

The cells of D-block are notoriously the most haunted cells in the prison. Pictured are the doorways to D13 and D14, both of which are inexplicably ice cold at all times.

building" (Babyak, 1988, p. 6). You shiver as you think about the feeling that this sound must have sent through the bodies of those men. Your eyes take a final sweep through the tiny dungeons. You do a double take—were those glowing red eyes that you just saw? You immediately turn away because that chill that won't go away is telling you that you really don't want to know.

Resuming the tour, you see the other spots throughout the island that are said to be haunted. There are so many of them that every step seems to find you facing the old story of a new ghost. Midway through your audio tour, you are asked to step outside. You can see the view of San Francisco from here, barely making out the distinct outlines of the city through the fog. You stand at the base of the famous lighthouse, which makes the island stand out when viewed from afar; the lighthouse that was constructed so diligently when the prison was being developed, the lighthouse that is said to be haunted.

Looking out from this spot, what catches your eye is the frighteningly choppy waters between you and the city. You eye the clouds circling above and hope that it isn't going to rain—imagining the chaos that this bay must turn into during a storm. Prison guard George Gregory had a shift in which he patrolled this island, probably passing regularly on this very spot where you now stand. He saw what these storms could do. As described by Babyak, the job of the island patrol officer was one that was generally not enjoyed. "His job at night was also repetitive and dreary. Using his flashlight sparingly, he began his rounds along the beach at the lower east end of the island. If it were a normal night, this was a tedious, silent, nagging cold vigil. Even on the leeward side of Alcatraz, the damp seeped through the woolen overcoats and dark, double-breasted suits with a vengeance. The patrolman's job was to surprise anyone or anything that trespassed. 'If you ever thought about spooks,' said Long (a patrolman interviewed by Babyak), 'that was the time to do it.'" This job also fell to new officers but they soon learned to distinguish between

A view of San Francisco from the prison at Alcatraz.

suspicious sounds and those of surf and seagulls. On more than one occasion, though, an officer skirmished with a yelping sea lion lolling up on the beach, or panicked upon stumbling over a thick, decomposed shark someone had hauled in and left to die" (Babyak, 1988, p. 26).

Guard George Gregory didn't scare easily and didn't think that he saw "spooks" out there...but he certainly knew that the nature of the area could be devastating. Describing the morning hours after a nightlong storm, he writes, "At the break of dawn, the wind died down and the torrents of rain diminished. With the coming of daylight, I became fascinated with the flotsam and jetsam stirred up by the storm. The bay was full of parts of buildings, trees, and a lot of other junk I couldn't identify. I saw a wide stream of muddy water that was easily distinguished from the gray of the bay water. As I watched, a huge timber came into view. It was being carried like a toothpick by the turbulent waters through the bay toward the open sea. Suddenly it went up on end to an almost vertical position, then down into the water out of sight" (Gregory, 2002, p. 62).

Standing here, suspended in time, you imagine what the bay could do to you if you fell off this island. Then, not wanting to imagine that horror anymore, you look back at the beautiful outline of the city of San Francisco. Like the prisoners who once were housed here, if the wind is just right, you can hear the sounds coming from the city. To the prisoners of Alcatraz, they must have considered this another form of torture. On your guided tour, you'll hear one of the old prisoners speaking about it, saying that on New Years Eve, laughter could always be heard nearby from the revelers in the city. But if you can hear the sounds of San Francisco as a tourist today, it is anything but taunting. It is comforting. Because if the wind isn't right, you may not hear San Francisco's activity; You may hear something

Left: **Standing at the base of the old lighthouse tower, it ominously looms above...**

else instead. And that something, which seems to have no source, is not something that you care to hear.

Amidst the calls of the birds, the whipping of the wind, and the chatter of the other travelers who have come to see Alcatraz with you, it may be difficult to discern what that other sound is. But if you can focus your mind for a moment, isolating the different sounds, you can hear something that doesn't quite sound familiar. Your audiotape may be turned off, but you can hear voices desperately trying to tell you their tale. When the sounds in the silence get too frightening, you can turn your audiotape back on and complete your tour.

Re-entering the building, your next stop will be the rooms that held the offices of the guards and the prison administration. As you look through the glass, take careful note of where everything is positioned. You probably won't see anything amiss as you check out your surroundings. But, if you were to return here later in the day, you might find that the typewriter has shifted or that the chair is no longer seated at the desk. Most people believe that the movement of the items is a prank that the security guards play on one another, but each of them swears that they haven't ever moved anything in that room. You probably won't want to know for sure, so you move on.

At the end of your audio tour, you may choose to remain on the island of Alcatraz for a while. There is an undeniable beauty about this place despite the ugliness that it has historically contained. And the plant life and bird nests that dot the island do have a certain appeal. But you have to admit that, as you make your way down to get in line for your ferry, you are none too sad to be leaving while there is still some sunlight illuminating the San Francisco skyline. As you file onto the boat, you stop at the snack bar. Out of the corner of your eye...you catch a movement to your left. You turn your head and swear that you see that shadow again, dancing at the edges of your vision, rattling the shackles on invisible ankles. The chill, if it ever left your body, lodges itself back in your spine. You place your order at the bar; you are ready for that drink *NOW*!

The prison administration offices, which you will see if you take a tour of Alcatraz. *Note: Take a copy of this photo on the tour and see whether any of the furnishings have moved as they reportedly do (with no known cause!).*

The HAUNTED Spots of Alcatraz

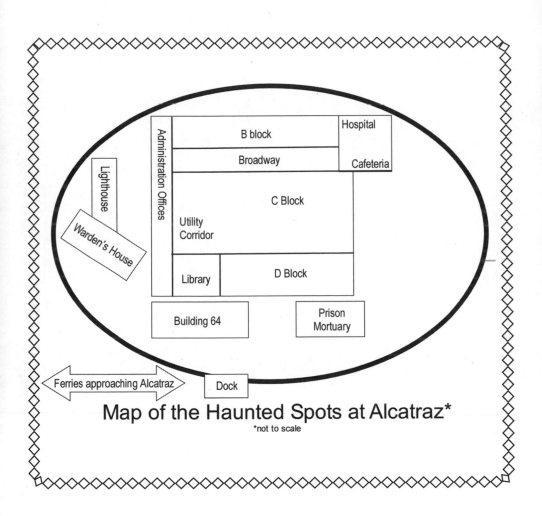

Map of the Haunted Spots at Alcatraz*
*not to scale

A Guide to the Haunted Locations

There ISN'T a Spot That's Safe...

The Cell Blocks

Inside the cell blocks of the federal prison, the compact location that you would explore if you were to take an audio tour of Alcatraz, are the locations where a majority of the spirits of Alcatraz are reported to be found. Ghost sightings and unsettling feelings are common throughout the entire cell house, from the wide-open library to the cafeteria kitchen, but it is the cell blocks, which were the homes of the prisoners, where ghosts are most commonly felt today. On Cell Block A, a loud scream is often heard by those standing at the bottom of the stairs. In Cell Block B, there is the old cell of Al Capone, who is said to haunt the building (although his ghost is most often heard in the shower room where he reportedly plays the banjo to this day).

There is a hallway between Cell Block B and Cell Block C—a hallway that you'll walk yourself if you take a tour of Alcatraz. The inmates of Alcatraz walked this hallway, known as "Broadway," daily. It was known as the place where the "fresh fish" (the newly arrived prisoners on Alcatraz) received the most taunting from their new peers as they walked to their cells for the first time. Because of this, it is known as a hallway where fear was prevalent, consistent, and abundant. Today, "park workers often report strange sounds echoing through the empty building as they walk down Broadway: coughs, laughs, whistles, the playing of a harmonica, and even the slamming of cell doors" (Ghost In My Suitcase, 2001-2006).

Tourists looking at the cells in the Alcatraz prison. Each hallway was its own block, alphabetically identified (as in A-block). Each held three tiers of cells.

Cell Block C is one of the more infamous cellblocks as far as the prison's ghostly history is concerned. It was explored by famous medium and psychic Sylvia Browne, who discovered the disembodied spirit of Abie "Butcher" Maldowitz in the deserted laundry room located there. This laundry room has also been reported to hold the ghosts of the past in the form of smoke. The room will fill with what looks like smoke from a fire, but then, when investigated, the smoke...just disappears. Not too far away, just off of Cell Block C, is the Utility Corridor where three prisoners who attempted to escape (Coy, Cretzer, and Hubbard) were ultimately captured and grenaded to their deaths. In this same corridor, a welded shut door muffles the eerie sounds of the spirits on this cellblock.

It is rumored that there have been other ghostly activities experienced in this same area. One of the most well-known incidents is a case that happened back in 1976. A guard who was watching the area at night heard odd noises coming from behind the door. It sounded as though something was knocking around in the corridor down there, but when the guard opened the door, he saw nothing that could possibly be making the sounds. He closed the door and was going to continue on his security rounds, but as soon as the door shut behind him, the noises started up again. Thinking that someone must be in there playing some sort of joke on him, the guard opened the door again and looked around the area extensively. He never found the source of the noise. When he closed the door again, the noises again resumed. He walked away as quickly as he could without breaking into a run. Since that time, this area has been blocked off and that particular door has been welded shut. (Taylor, 2006)

But the most infamous of all of the Cell Blocks is Cell Block D. This was the area where the isolation cells were located (sometimes known as treatment unit cells and strip cells, but most commonly referred to, ominously and accurately, as *"THE HOLE"*). Numerous modern day visitors to the island have reported feeling icy fingers on the backs of their necks when they were exploring these cells as part of their guided tours of the island. And cell D14 is the cell that holds the ghost most often reported by everyone who says they've seen spirits on the island...the ghost of Rufe McCain.

The Hospital

You won't see this part of the prison during your tour of Alcatraz since it is closed to the general public, but Alcatraz tour guides and security staff have often thought tourists had wandered into this area because of the noises they would hear from here during tours. "More than once a ranger has heard voices and movement and dashed upstairs to escort trespassers out of the hospital area, only to find it deserted" (Ghost In My Suitcase, 2001-2006).

Maybe what they're hearing is the ghost of Robert "Birdman" Stroud, a prisoner who left Alcatraz while still alive but who is reported to have returned to haunt the island, reportedly remaining there to this day. The cries of living birds on the island can't cover the distinctive whistling birdcall that some say they still hear The Birdman making. And though these calls are heard all over the island, the hospital was home to some of the darkest days of isolation for Robert Stroud and is where a bulk of his pain is held. Perhaps his soul is captured there as well.

Or perhaps those souls left there belong to the many other men who received treatment for physical and mental ailments during their stay at Alcatraz—men whose voices are reportedly still heard there to this day. "The National Park staff has reported odd sounds floating down the stairway, and a few have even seen hazy apparitions" (Ghost In My Suitcase, 2001-2006). And more than one person has heard the whispering ghost of a dead inmate say curiously, "I feel good."

Prison Administration Offices

During the time that they were in operation, the prison administration offices were a rather dull place to spend time. And for the most part, they remain dull today. During your tour, you'll be able to look in them, through glass, to see the desks and phones that were used when this was an active prison. But if you look carefully, you might see some shifting of the furniture in the room. It is said that the chair, which is usually displayed at the main desk, often winds up in different locations of the room. And occasionally, the typewriter is shifted to a different spot on the desk. Most people believe that the security guards who keep an eye on the tourists of Alcatraz are just moving things around as a prank to pass the time and frighten their co-workers. But everyone who works there insists that they have nothing to do with the movement.

The Cafeteria

Tour guides will tell you that the cafeteria was one of the inmates' favorite places. The food served was generally good, following mandates by the wardens and prison regulations. Eating good food is a pleasure for anyone and anything that appeals to the senses has got to be good for inmates who experience monotony day in and day out. But this was also a place where a large number of prisoners would be held together at one time, and so there was always tension and fear. Riots took place, knives stolen from the kitchen were later used in assaults, and daily troubles were common. Perhaps they are still being settled. "Today, when the tourists are gone and the cell block is quiet, park rangers have

The cafeteria was a favorite place of the prisoners, but it was also where several acts of violence occurred.

heard the muffled sounds of voices and the clanking of silverware coming from the empty cafeteria" (Ghost In My Suitcase, 2001-2006).

Warden Johnston's House

Although there were four different wardens during the time that Alcatraz was a federal prison, Warden Johnston is often the one people think of when they think of the warden of Alcatraz. And his old home on the island *IS* a place said to be filled with spirits. In fact, although Warden Johnston reportedly did not believe in ghosts, he experienced unsettling events of his own here that made him think that something otherworldly could be taking place on Alcatraz. Maybe you can get the full story from the woman who can be heard sobbing from behind the dungeon walls located near Johnston's old home. Or perhaps it is a story better told by the man with the muttonchops who appeared to guards here in the mid-twentieth century. (Ghost In My Suitcase, 2001–2006)

The Exercise Yard

Warden Johnston was hardly the only person on the island to see ghost activity before the inmates of Alcatraz came back to haunt the island. Some of the ghosts that linger on the island today were there at the time that it was a federal prison, sighted by the inmates who were stuck there. Most of these ghosts were believed to be Civil War soldiers. Nearly fifty of these soldiers were reported to have died on Alcatraz and it is said that they sometimes showed up in line with the inmates during counts of prisoners in the exercise yard (Ghost in My Suitcase, 2001-2006). Count was taken when the prisoners were about to enter the yard and as they were about to leave, and often, when the prisoners would line up for count before heading back to their cells, the count would be off. Extra men, dressed not in prison uniforms but rather in old military uniforms, would be present in the line, always disappearing when a recount was done by the guards (Ghost In My Suitcase, 2001-2006).

The Sally Port

The cell house may be where prisoners were famous for spending their days and nights, but it wasn't the home of the original prisoners of Alcatraz. The cell house wasn't built until the time when Alcatraz was a punitive, maximum-security federal prison. Prior to that, the island was a military prison, which held incarcerated individuals in dank conditions. Soldiers, Confederate prisoners of the Civil War, and others captured by the military were held in dungeons in the basement of The Sally Port building. No one can say for sure what happened to them while they lived in these conditions, but many say that their spirits still suffer here. (Ghost In My Suitcase, 2001–2006)

Building 64

You'll inevitably see this building on any tour that you take of Alcatraz, passing by it as you make your way up to the cell house where so many of the island's ghosts are said to be located. It is fenced off so that you can't go near it, with signs warning you away for *"your own safety."* Is this because the old buildings are falling apart and the United States National Park Service wants to make sure that you don't damage them and, in doing so, cause harm to your physical self? Or is it because the ghosts that are said to still haunt this location may do damage to your psychological self beyond what the park is willing to acknowledge?

During its active days, Building 64 was first a military barracks. It later served as the housing for the guards who worked at the federal prison on the island and their families who resided there with them. This area of the island was not necessarily an unhappy area. In fact, children who grew up there often recount their life here as being mostly pleasant. "Still, Building 64 has been the site of some paranormal activity. A security guard that works for the park system described staying there at night as "creepy." While spending the night in the building, the rangers' audio snapped into life, blaring a slow, garbled version of the tourist presentation" (Ghost In My Suitcase, 2001-2006).

Prison Mortuary

The prison mortuary was never a pleasant place. After all, it was one of the final stops for the bodies of those who died while serving out their sentences on this harshest of islands. And so, it is no surprise that spirits are said to haunt this spot. But exactly whose spirits are stuck there may come as a surprise. There have never been reports by anyone visiting Alcatraz that there are ghosts of prison inmates haunting this location. But there have been reports of sounds that are described as the cries of a little girl.

Tourists encounter this spot as they walk up towards the cell house, frequently stopping to take photographs here. As they crouch down to look into the underground room, their attention is sometimes caught by what sounds like slight sobbing. Listening more closely, they can make out the definitive sound of a young girl crying. One visitor reported seeing a small child standing at the corner of the room, with her back to the tourists. He said that the glean of her hair indicated that she was a young Native American child and that the clothing she wore appeared to come from 1970s America. Although there are no reports of children dying during the years

of Native American activist occupation on the island, these reports bring up the question of what remains undocumented and untold from that time in the history of the island of Alcatraz.

The Lighthouse

It's not just the lighthouse that exists today that is said to be haunted, although spirits reportedly linger in the fog here. Additionally, a second lighthouse is said to appear sometimes in the midst of the fog. Who is it trying to guide home?

Left: This is the old mortuary for prisoners who died during their time at Alcatraz. The table for their bodies is empty now, but a young Native American girl reportedly hides in the corner shadows, sobbing.

Part III:

The Prisoners Who Haunt Alcatraz

A Ghostly Roll Call

People flock from all over the world to visit the famous tourist attractions of San Francisco, with one of the biggest draws being Alcatraz Island. Travelers board the ferries in hordes to take advantage of the opportunity to learn about the rich history of the infamous prison located just over a mile out in the San Francisco Bay. The fascination with the area is caused by a combination of a number of different factors, not the least of which is the morbid interest of individuals in the intensity and drama surrounding lives that were riddled with crime.

In a time when it is possible to buy trading cards featuring serial killers, to consider watching executions on television, and to be frightened to the bone by Hollywood dramatizations of real life crime stories, the human interest in the daily lives of the most hardened criminals is insatiable. It has been this way for some time, which is why the initial opening of the federal prison on Alcatraz drew so much national media attention. People wanted to know more about the prisoners who were said to have been so horrible that they had to be sent to this most punishing of institutions.

Perhaps because of this fascination and the hype that surrounded the lives of the most infamous prisoners of Alcatraz, it is believed by many that the ghosts remaining on the island today belong to those who were most well-known during their living stints there. Maybe this is just because people want to believe that their trip to Alcatraz may allow them to brush up against a little bit of the infamy that made the place so well known. But maybe...it is more than some wishful fabrication of the mind. Perhaps the prisoners who were able to gain notoriety during their lives at Alcatraz were not quite ready to relinquish this fame for the quiet lack of recognition in the afterlife when that time was supposed to come.

Perhaps it is even more complex than this. It is impossible to say what causes a spirit to linger in any given location. Surely, one motivating factor is the series of tragic events surrounding an untimely death. The prison of Alcatraz certainly had its fair share of tragedy and the people who lived life there were so haunted in life that maybe they felt compelled to haunt others once they'd died. The reasons for ghosts to stick around are as many and varied as the individuals who research ghost activity and derive theories about the spirit world.

Whether or not you believe that the famous prisoners of Alcatraz continue to walk the halls of the prison to this day, it is certainly undeniable that these folks left their marks on the prison walls. They are the reason why travelers from remote locations take an interest in exploring the cells of the old prison. They are the faces that remain in your mind when the whole history of Alcatraz is explained to you. They are the spirits that generate an interest in the island.

It is the most famous prisoners of Alcatraz...that have become the most famous of Alcatraz ghosts. Say that it's all celebrity hype if you will, but when you wander through the self-guided tour and hear the low strum of Al Capone's guitar or sense the unseemly chill emanating from the cell of Robert "Birdman" Stroud, you might have some trouble explaining the source of your disbelief.

Famous Prisoners

Robert "Birdman" Stroud

Still Shrieking in the Wind....

The "Birdman of Alcatraz" is one of the most notorious prisoners in the short history of the federal prison, gaining international and timeless notice as a result of media attention to the study of ornithology, which he completed during his time as an inmate. Interestingly, although Stroud is most commonly associated with being "The Birdman" and is most commonly linked with the time he spent incarcerated on Alcatraz, his studies of birds took place off the island, before his transfer there from his prison home of Leavenworth. This discrepancy is a perfect example of how truth and fiction tend to blend in the re-telling of the history of Alcatraz. Between the actual truth, the loss of details over time, and the fabrications of the media (in this case it was a movie about Stroud that placed his bird studies at Alcatraz[4]), it is hard to say what "really" happened on the island.

The accuracy of some of the details just can't be known. But what can be known is that Robert "Birdman" Stroud was a hardened criminal who ended up at Alcatraz because of his violent actions. In the beginning of his criminal career, he was really just a common violent criminal. Stroud was in Alaska when he committed a brutal murder and was sentenced to a dozen years in the federal penitentiary at Leavenworth. He served nearly all of his time and could have gone on his merry way except for the fact that, just prior to his release, he attacked and murdered a Leavenworth prison guard. Though sentenced to death at that time, Stroud's sentence was commuted to life in solitary confinement by President Wilson, who was interested in the ornithological work that was being done in Stroud's cell (Smith, 2004, p. 174-176).

The whole bird thing had started innocently enough. Stroud had found a sparrow in the exercise yard at Leavenworth and taken it back to his cell and nursed it until it could thrive. This sparked the interest in birds and he began to correspond with as many bird societies as he could. Some of them complied with his requests for information and he began to study in earnest, becoming something of an expert on the topic. In fact, he wrote a book, *Stroud's Digest of the Diseases of Birds*, based upon the information he had gathered together from his correspondence (Heaney, 1987, p. 96). It was this work that had impressed President Wilson.

But not all of the people who came into contact with him during his years in prison would be similarly impressed. In fact, the people at Leavenworth considered him mostly a bother because his work with the birds encouraged the problem of other inmates wanting their own pets. Pressure by the bird societies kept him with his birds at Leavenworth for a time, but eventually, the prison got tired of the problem. "They woke him up in the middle of the night and bundled him off without his birds" (Heaney, 1987, p. 97).

He was sent to Alcatraz in 1942.

The people who worked with Stroud at Alcatraz were much more like the guards and administration of Leavenworth in their assessment of Robert Stroud than they were like President Wilson. In his biographical account of working as a guard at Alcatraz, George Gregory relays a conversation he had with Stroud, which gives insight into the Birdman's mental state. He describes Stroud as someone who would frequently espouse on educational or informational topics, speaking as though he was an authority on the subject but who, when tested by an actual authority, would prove to know little to nothing about the field of which he was speaking. For example, Gregory describes a time when a French-speaking priest visited Alcatraz

Are the birds that are on Alcatraz Island today still communicating
with Robert "Birdman" Stroud?

and Gregory asked him to speak with Stroud in French. The reason for this was that Stroud had made a great impression upon people because he had learned to speak French in six short weeks during his incarceration on the island. As it turned out, when the priest spoke to Stroud in French, Stroud had no idea what the priest was saying. He continued to pretend as though he understood the priest, but it became readily apparent to Gregory and those watching the situation that Stroud was nothing but a fake. (Gregory, 2002, p. 88-90)

Gregory goes on to say that the same was true of Stroud's study of ornithology. He got many books on the subject and could speak at great length about birds, but he would pretend that he was speaking from his own first hand research when really he was just reciting what he'd learned from his books. Gregory reports that he heard from guards who worked at Leavenworth when Stroud studied birds there that the birds were part of an elaborate plot to get alcohol into the prison. Stroud would request alcohol for use on the slides he was using to study birds, but he would actually drink the alcohol and not use it for any bird studies. (Gregory, 2002, p. 88–90)

It's impossible to say whether Stroud was always this way – manipulative, conniving, and probably a liar – or whether it was the years of being institutionalized that caused his pathology. What is much easier to say with relative certainty is that the years that The Birdman spent at Alcatraz surely caused at least some deterioration of his mental state, regardless of what that state might have been to begin with. It was inevitable really, since Stroud was always kept in isolation. "An administrative decision made by an assistant attorney general required that Stroud be confined in segregation for the rest of his life" (Gregory, 2002, p. 37).

That kind of ongoing isolation would be enough to make even the sanest person go a little bit crazy. It is the kind of thing that is conducive to mental deterioration from the inside out. And it is the kind of thing that is so traumatic that a spirit might get stuck in the place that it happened. Such is said to be the case with Robert "Birdman" Stroud. "Eventually the Birdman was released from Alcatraz, but since his death in 1963 visitors to the island have been hearing Stroud's distinctive whistle attempting to reach his beloved birds from beyond the grave" (Smith, 2004, p. 174-176).

As a visitor to the island today, it is hard to find any sort of silence. There are so many people around you visiting the attraction that the chatter and laughter and inquisitive queries keep otherworldly sounds at bay. But the sound that you will notice most frequently at Alcatraz, the one that you simply cannot ignore, is the sound of the birds that are circling and landing all around you during your stay. And if you pay close attention to this sound, blocking out the rest of the island's cacophony, what you may hear is a kind of call-and-response. One side of that sound is the birds. But the other side is a strange whistle. Is the "Birdman" still seeking to appease his lonely sense of isolation by calling his old bird friends? Or are the birds trying to call to his soul, which may remain stuck in the hospital where so many of his years of isolation occurred?

Al Capone

The Banjo's Mournful Tune....

The Birdman may have been famous for the ornithological work he did once he was in prison, but there were definitely some prisoners who were famous specifically for the acts that landed them in prison. One of the major players in terms of this kind of prisoner was Al Capone. His face served as the message to the public that the Department of Justice was trying to portray with the opening of the federal prison at Alcatraz.

"Al Capone is America's best known gangster and the single greatest symbol of the collapse of law and order in the United States during the 1920s Prohibition era" (Chicago Historical Society, 1999). This new kind of crime boss that had sprung up during Prohibition and spread throughout the Depression Era was not going to be tolerated and people like Al Capone were going to be punished.

Capone was the kind of criminal that you you imagine when you think of someone with a long personal history of committing crimes. His deviations from acceptable behavior began when he was just a kid. He was born in Brooklyn, New York at the turn of the nineteenth century (obviously not the easiest of cities or times in which to learn to behave appropriately in society). The kind of neighborhood bonding that was required to survive in a neighborhood like the one Capone grew up in lent itself well to gang affiliation. By the time he was fourteen (the year that he dropped out of school), Capone had racked up membership in two neighborhood "kid gangs": the Brooklyn Rippers and the Forty Thieves Juniors. Eventually, Capone would join the Five Points Gang in Manhattan (Chicago Historical Society, 1999).

His gang activity led him to commit murders and brutal assaults. In accordance with gang code, everyone in the neighborhood was keeping silent about these events, so it took some time for the police to catch up with Capone. During that time, he engaged in numerous street and bar fights, one of which caused disfiguring scars on his face, leading to his infamous nickname, "Scarface." Although his gang activity hadn't yet caught up with him legally, he was creating quite a stir in New York to the point where his gang boss moved him to Chicago to let things "cool down."

Capone's life in Chicago would take books to chronicle, but the story can be boiled down to a quick summary. He lived the life of a major crime boss, moving up in the ranks and taking over the city's underground activity. He ran saloons, collected gambling debts, and involved himself in the murders and assaults of countless people. He gained the respect of his crew and eventually ran the area for a time. Undoubtedly, he made many enemies. And having enemies means always living in fear. Capone's heart was surely filling with this constant sense of being on guard.

It was 1931 when Al Capone was arrested. It wasn't for murder or for any of the other major activities in which he had engaged. It was for income tax evasion and ultimately for "conspiracy to violate Prohibition laws from 1922–31" (Chicago Historical Society, 1999). It was from this sentence that he was sent to prison in Chicago. Of course, we all know that big criminals have their connections both inside and outside of prison. Capone continued to run his crime ring from prison. Because this was widely known and because Capone had gained so much notoriety in the media for his actions, he was selected for transfer to Alcatraz when it opened. In other words, Capone was meant to set an example.

It is said that Capone's criminal activity indeed subsided when he was moved to Alcatraz. "He was unable to control anyone or anything and could not buy influence or friends. In an attempt to earn time off for good behavior, Capone became the ideal prisoner and refused to participate in prisoner rebellions or strikes" (Chicago Historical Society, 1999). But all was not pretty during his time at Alcatraz. Capone began to suffer the symptoms of dementia caused by a case of syphilis. His mind and body both began to deteriorate during his time at Alcatraz. Much of his prison sentence was served out in the prison's hospital.

Capone did indeed serve his sentence. Despite his high-profile image, Capone was one of those prisoners who did his time and was released. It is said that he lived a quiet life upon release until his death in 1947. But perhaps all of that fear he'd lived with for so many long years made it impossible for Capone to simply go and rest on the other side of life because it is said that Capone still haunts Alcatraz to this day.

An employee who once worked at the park reported that he heard the strumming of a guitar coming from the shower room. At the time, the employee didn't know that Capone was famous among the prisoners for spending his days hiding out in this area of the prison, playing his banjo (Taylor, 2006). He may have been trying to drown out the voices of the past that were ricocheting in his own head. Although the park employee didn't know about this, he soon learned the story because others came forward to say that they, too, had heard this banjo playing despite the fact that Capone had long been gone from the prison. Why return in spirit to Alcatraz, a prison that was supposed to be one of the harshest in existence at its time? Perhaps Capone was able to rest at Alcatraz in a way that he couldn't when he was out on the streets. Perhaps Alcatraz was a sort of refuge for him in that way.

And maybe he just couldn't bring himself to leave the prison. Perhaps he finds some sort of comfort in the afterlife, sitting inside of that shower room where he found some refuge from the rest of prison life. Maybe he remains there still. The tour guides who have reported that they sometimes hear his banjo playing throughout the empty building after the tourists have gone for the day certainly think that this is possible. And it is not just the banjo that indicates that Capone may still be around. American Paranormal researchers took a tour of Alcatraz in 2003 and reported that they were able to capture on film two orbs located near Cell 133 on B-Block, the cell that was home to Al Capone when he was not being hospitalized. According to their reports on the orbs, "The one on the right is round, beautifully white and dense. No possibility of reflection or other camera or manmade artifact exists. The "orb" does show up on the negative. There is also an "orb" on the left at approximately the third "room" door at approximately the halfway point" (American Paranormal Investigators, 2003).

Additionally, amateur reports support the belief of ghost activity in Capone's old cell. Reportedly, a contractor once spent the night in Capone's old cell. "He was very scared to stay there, but was also very curious. Once he decided to settle in, and try to get some sleep it took many hours until he began to finally doze off, when he was awoken by some sort of a banging noise. It began far away, and got closer and closer. He said it was as if a security guard was walking along, banging his club on the bars. The noise got closer and closer until it stopped right in front of the cell he was in and then he heard several very loud bangs on the bars of the cell and then it all just stopped. Needless to say he never was able to fall asleep that night. He lie awake the whole night and was out of there on the first ferry the next morning" (Katie, 2005).

Of course, this is one of those stories in which fiction and fact have blended over time. Some say that no one has ever spent the night on Alcatraz so this latter tale could not be true. But others insist that they've taken these tours, seen the orbs and heard that banjo playing in the night. There's no way to say for sure what kind of spirit haunts the island or why Al Capone would return here after being released and dying as a free man. But there's also no way to say for sure that the banjo *isn't* playing in the shower room today.

Roy Gardner

Haunted by Hellcatraz....

"Quick with a gun, controversial, no prison could hold him — these were the words used in talking about Roy Gardner" (Kelly, 2007). As the latter part of this description indicates, Gardner was a man who was known for his ability to escape from any number of prisons and situations of incarceration. Eventually all of the trouble that he caused escaping from tight-security prisons would land him at Alcatraz. Of course, he would not escape from the "escape-proof" prison. But he would eventually serve his time and leave the prison, after which he wrote his autobiography: *Hellcatraz*.

The name of the book reflects the horrid conditions on Alcatraz. And it's a name that has stuck over time although many people have forgotten the story of Roy Gardner. It's a sad story to be forgotten since it is filled with all of the richest aspects of a good twentieth century crime story. It includes train robberies, prison escapes, and a Hollywood-type of love story. Not to mention the fact that the "bad guy" eventually publishes his story and receives a modicum of local fame. But the fame wouldn"t be enough to keep Gardner alive despite the fact that he became a free man.

Gardner was most known during his lifetime for his "great escapes." In the early days of his career, he quickly became legendary for these escapes. For example, at the beginning of the twentieth century, Gardner went "to Arizona where he purchased a wagon and a team of mules and went into the business of smuggling arms and ammunition to the army of rebels attempting to overthrow the Mexican government" (Kelly, 2007). Once caught, he was sentenced to death. "Taken to prison he was tossed into a dungeon and left for several days in solitary confinement and total darkness. When he was judged to have reached the breaking point, he was dragged to the torture chamber, where cords were tightened in the manner of a tourniquet until his body grew numb. Early one morning when the guard brought him his breakfast, Gardner had disappeared like a Poltergeist" (Kelly, 2007).

His ability to get in and out of situations helped his penchant for crime, and the rest of his life would continue with crimes committed and eventually time served for them, with escapes spattered in between. In the midst of this, he met and fell in love with a woman named Dolly. In the true blindness of romance, she couldn't see anything bad about her man. And so she vowed to stick by his side through thick and thin, a vow she kept for a considerably long period of time considering how in-and-out of prison Gardner was (Kelly, 2007).

By the mid 1920s, Gardner had racked up enough escapes to his name to be known as the "King of the Escape Artists." So when he was caught again, he was sent to Leavenworth. He "tried umpteen times to escape from Leavenworth but each time his attempts were thwarted" (Kelly, 2007). He was transferred to Atlanta because the warden was afraid he would escape from Leavenworth. And from Atlanta, he was taken to Alcatraz with the first group of prisoners to be sent to the island.

Gardner spent four years at Alcatraz and was then paroled. He wrote *Hellcatraz*, which gained him some local notoriety of a kind better than that he'd received throughout his life of crime. But the attention wasn't good enough to resolve the heartbreak that had come his way. For, although his girl had remained true to him for a while, she had eventually given up on Gardner and had married someone else during the time he was at Alcatraz (Kelly, 2007).

Ultimately, Gardner couldn't stand the heartache. In 1940, he was found in his motel room, dead by suicide. He "dropped a couple of cyanide pellet in a glass of acid (the way it's done in executions at San Quentin), covered his head with a towel, and breathed in the fumes" (Heaney, 1987, p. 93). He left a suicide note that said that he was old and tired and didn't want to spend any more of his days struggling with life (Heaney, 1987, p. 93). Apparently Gardner, the man who could escape from almost anywhere, couldn't escape his own life. Although he had served his time at Alcatraz and then was released, he seems to have made the island his permanent home. Maybe after a life in and out of lock up, he knows no other place to be.

Or at least, it's his spirit to which the sound of tunneling beneath the cellblocks is often attributed. Gardner was known for his ability to tunnel through almost anything. He was quiet about it of course so you can't hear him very often. But every once in awhile, when the wind is more still than usual, there is a scratching underneath the ground. If you manage to steal away from the rest of the tour group, you can stand in one of the cellblock hallways and hear this sound beneath your feet, traveling away from you, this sound that supposedly belongs to the late Roy Gardner.

Those Who Tried to Escape Alcatraz

And Found There Was NO Escaping....

Some prisoners, like Al Capone, were infamous for the activities they engaged in, which landed them at Alcatraz. Others, like Stroud, became known more for the activities they engaged in during the time they were imprisoned. And then there are those prisoners who may or may not have been known inside prison walls for their activities, but who became famous among people on the outside for their attempts to leave Alcatraz—attempts that always failed in one form or another.

Alcatraz was known as a prison from which there was no escape. First of all, the security on the prison grounds was intense. Guards were trained to watch the inmates carefully and the regimen was strict to prevent any problems. But even if the guards failed at their duty, the position of Alcatraz in the bay made escape nearly impossible. The waters there are harsh and difficult to navigate even with the best of equipment. And they are cold, icy cold. A prisoner wearing only prison-issued clothes would be unlikely to survive in the conditions of the Bay water.

But that didn't stop people from trying. Numerous prisoners tried to escape over the years. And some of them tried so hard...and then failed...that perhaps their spirits remain stuck there to this day. They are within the walls of the prison, trying to figure out what went wrong during the course of their great scheme and how they're going to escape. There are four incidents of escaping prisoners that have led to ghosts on the island. The first prisoner to ever try to escape from the island is said to still be there today. In another case case, it was a night watchman whose spirit became stuck during the course of the events. In the third story, a bloody situation that ended in the deaths of both guards and escapees resulted in the haunting of the island by more than one ghost. And in the final case, the disappearance of the escapees into seemingly thin air left a vacuum for a ghost to remain.

Joe Bowers

Joe Bowers was a name that eventually became known because of his attempts to escape Alcatraz. The name is also synonymous with death. Before this attempted escape, Bowers slit his throat in an early suicide attempt. And later, in his final escape attempt, Bowers was shot and killed on the fence of the grounds of Alcatraz. It is believed that his spirit is one of the ones that remain trapped on Alcatraz today.

Bowers was one of the first prisoners to be transferred to Alcatraz. In 1935, the year following this transfer, he attempted suicide at the prison. He had broken his eyeglasses and used a piece of the glass to slit his throat; the attempt was unsuccessful and he sustained only minor injuries (GAzis-Sax, 1997). It was determined that he was faking suicidal behavior to try to be transferred off of Alcatraz. When that didn't work, Bowers tried to escape.

It was the following year, 1936, when the escape attempt occurred. Bowers had recently come from three months spent in the dungeons of the prison after a series of fights landed him there for solitary confinement. When he was released from the dungeons, he was given a job at the incinerator. It was here that the escape attempt occurred—although, the truth of that depends on who is telling the story. It is possible that Bowers was on the fence solely for the purpose of feeding some of the seagulls at Alcatraz. But the guard who saw him on the fence didn't think so...he pulled out his gun and fatally shot Joseph Bowers (GAzis-Sax, 1997). Reportedly, the guard "was aiming to hit him in the legs. But the force was so great that Bowers fell over the side of the cliff and down to the rocks below. He died from his injuries in the fall" (Heaney, 1987, p. 101).

Bowers had no shortage of mental health problems during the time he was incarcerated at Alcatraz. His time in the dungeons only served to worsen that condition. And so maybe this is why his spirit became stuck there. For, after his death, other inmates who were sent to the dungeons swore that they could hear him telling his story there. Over and over again, Bowers insisted that he was "just trying to feed the birds." He's apparently been feeding them for a long, long time.

Mr. Cline

In his memoir as an Alcatraz prison guard, George Gregory describes one of the escapes he was told about during his initial tour of the island. He writes:

"Ken unlocked the door to a building that sat right at the edge of the water. He listened, shone his flashlight around, and said, "We call this the old work area. The industrial shops are now farther along the island and this building is used only for storage." He shone his light on the wall phone and directed the beam down the wall.

"Can you see those marks?"

"Yes."

"Those are the bloody marks of Mr. Cline's hands. He passed out trying to reach the telephone to sound the alarm on what became one of the bloodiest escape attempts on Alcatraz. He died later as a result of his wounds.

"Three convicts succeeded in making an escape after they bludgeoned Mr. Cline with a hammer. They went out through a window and up the side of the building to the roof. Mr. Stites had just come on duty in the Model Tower, which was near the place the convicts came up on the roof. He grabbed his .45 and shot one of them in the forehead, killing him instantly. Stites hit the next one in the shoulder while he was trying to get through the barbed wire and back down the building. A second bullet shot him in the other shoulder, so he gave up. Seeing the trouble they were in, the third convict dived under the tower. He was soon in the Hole" (Gregory, 2002, p. 65–66).

The marks from Mr. Cline's hands still remain on the wall of the tower. And that's not all that remains. It is rumored that there is occasionally the sound of scuffling heading up to the roof of this area. A phantom shot can be heard and then the scuffle is over. If you were to hear it, you'd probably figure that your imagination was playing tricks on you or that the sound of the wind in the air created the movement you heard. But if you know the story about Mr. Cline, you know that the battle between prisoner and guard is long from over.

Coy, Cretzer, and Hubbard

The most famous of the Alcatraz escape attempts could very well be the case of Coy, Cretzer, and Hubbard. An audio tour of Alcatraz today will take you through the history of this case, but it is famous for other reasons as well. It is famous because it was such an elaborate escape attempt. It is famous because it was so bloody and violent...it led to the deaths of guards as well as of the prisoners who tried to leave. And it is famous because of the number of people who swear that the ghosts of those involved in this battle remain in the prison to this day.

The year was 1946. It was May, and the escape attempt lasted over the course of three days from May 2 to May 4. On May 2, "six men by the names of Bernard Coy, Joseph Cretzer, Sam Shockley, Clarence Carnes, Marvin Hubbard, and Miran Thompson, took control of the cell house. Overpowering officers and gaining access to weapons and keys, they planned to escape through the recreation yard door. However, when they found they didn't have the key to the outside door, they decided to fight rather than giving up" (Legends of America, 2003–2007).

That day and the following two days were filled with fear and violence. The men managed to lock several guards into two adjoining cells. Two of these guards would be fatally shot before the days were over. Everyone on the cell blocks feared for their lives since no one knew for sure what turns would be taken by the men. Ultimately, the United States Marines were called in to help take control of the prison. The three men who originally set up the plan — Coy, Cretzer, and Hubbard — hid out in the utility corridor. Grenades thrown into the area caused their deaths.

Apparently, the three men were never able to escape Alcatraz, not even in death, for it is said that they continue to haunt the utility corridor to this day. "The restless spirits of the three have been reported numerous times at the utility door" (Ghost In My Suitcase, 2001-2006). One of the most often-recounted tales is the story of a guard who patrolled the prison grounds in the 1970s when the prison was no longer active in any way. He heard noises coming from this area, but found nothing there when he went to check it out. The source of the noises was never determined, but the door was eventually welded shut, perhaps to contain the spirits that might have been stirring up the ruckus!

And it is not only the escapees who lost their souls to Alcatraz during this bloodiest of escape attempts. Two guards died in the cells during the time they were being held hostage by the prisoners. It is believed that one or both of them remain stuck in the area today. After all, that is the only explanation for how the signage in the exhibits today which details the history of the escape attempt regularly gets moved around when no one is there to enter the cells.

Frank Lee Morris & the Anglin brothers

One of the most elaborate escape attempts on the prison, and the one that came the closest to being successful, was that of Frank Lee Morris and brothers Clarence and John Anglin. This escape is, again, one of the most famous of all of the escape attempts on the island. That's because this one actually resulted in the prisoners going missing. And although it is said that they died in the frigid waters of the bay, it isn't known for sure where their bodies (or their spirits) ultimately ended up.

The escape was actually planned by another man, Allen C. West, who recognized that the deteriorating state of the prison was conducive to planning and executing an escape. "Prisoners, as well as others, could see the deterioration in the cell house; cracks appeared frequently and cornices fell off — but it was doubtful West knew that the ventilation frills in the back of the cells had been made smaller when the Feds took over in 1934. And it wasn't even known by officials that work crews apparently hadn't reinforced the cement around the cents with steel rods or wire mesh. The erosion may have been apparent in the utility corridor" (Babyak, 1988, p. 104).

That erosion made it relatively easy to start cutting away at the building's interior. "According to prison and FBI reports of items found in the prisoners' cells, the quartet used hack saw blades, scraps of serrated tin, six-inch homemade chisels with taped handles, and table utensils with sharpened edges. Some officers thought the men used star drills that they had found after re-plumbing the cell house, but none were listed in the reports. They worked at night, beginning in September of 1961, digging first one hole, then another, until they had twenty or thirty and could chip away larger chunks of the cement. To hide the increasingly large holes, Clarence Anglin made fake cardboard ventilator frills with simulated concrete to fit over the enlarged vents. Towels hanging down from their sinks also hid the openings" (Babyak, 1988, p. 104-105).

In addition to the elaborate deconstruction of the interior of Alcatraz, the escapees worked on other parts of the plan to make sure that all went well. Clarence Anglin made dummy masks out of materials including soap chips, plaster, and human hair. These masks were placed in the beds of the cells of the men so that guards doing the count would think that they were still in their beds. Additionally, the men made life jackets, a life preserver, and a raft out of any materials that they could get their hands on. They were nothing if not resourceful. "Later FBI examination of a homemade life preserver left atop the cell block showed ingenuity. Using rubber-backed cotton raincoats, they not only sewed the seams, but also used hot steam pipes to vulcanize them, making them — they hoped — airtight. They also used spray bottle tops to inflate the jackets. West admitted getting the ideas from the magazines that slipped through the censors" (Babyak, 1988, p. 105).

It was the middle of June in 1962 when the escape took place. The two Anglin brothers and Morris were present for the nighttime head count that took place just after 9 p.m.; immediately following this, they made their move. They opened up the vents and entered them, moving up the utility shafts to the upper levels of the prison and eventually to the prison's roof. Once there, they scuttled down pipes that laced the side of the prison building. They made it to the ground and then ascended again, this time to climb over the fence that surrounded the prison. They had their homemade rafts and life vests with them and they inflated them, set them into the water, and made their escape. This is all that is known about their final moments on Alcatraz Island, information that was pieced together when a search was done to find the inmates. They were never able to tell their side of the story since they were never found.

No one really knows for sure what happened to the men who escaped that night. Since they were never heard from, there's the chance that they managed to successfully escape from Alcatraz. But it is commonly accepted that it is far more likely that they died in the waters surrounding the haunted island. It is commonly believed that no one has really escaped from Alcatraz. And indeed, it seems that they were unable to leave the island entirely. At night sometimes, security guards patrolling the island have heard a scratching sound. It has been described as possibly sounding like cardboard scraping across the ventilation grates.

As for West, he didn't escape that night. "He claimed his fake grill had been cemented so tight he was unable to loosen it that night, but he repeatedly acknowledged fear of the water" (Babyak, 1988, p. 106–107). Maybe he was right to feel such fear. It has been reported that there is sometimes the sound of splashing in the water...which can't be attributed to any visible force. Sure, it's usually dismissed as the sound of the waves slapping against the island rocks or perhaps a bird swooping down close to the water. But no one really knows for sure what the sound is...just like no one really knows for sure what happened to Frank Morris and the Anglin brothers the night of their escape.

Ghosts Without A Name or Fame

Some of the spirits of Alcatraz, like The Birdman and Al Capone, were famous in life and remained famous in death. Other ghosts that are said to haunt Alcatraz are known by name today, but were nameless in their lifetimes, merely numbers on the rosters used for roll call during the prison's active years. Some of them are spirits that we know by name today only because they were rediscovered in their deaths by the researchers who tried to find answers about the ghosts haunting Alcatraz. Rufe McCain and Abie "Butcher" Maldowitz are two such spirits.

Then, there are the ghosts that have no name, neither in life nor in death. Though someone once loved them enough to name them and care for them, their personal histories are lost to time. Today, we only know of their existence because of their insistence on making it known. The unexplainable

This is a typical cell at Alcatraz. The average person's arm span could reach from wall to wall.

The average cellmate might have items in his cell that included books, drawings he'd done, photographs, and shaving tools.

chills in the prison cells, the strange sounds that sometimes can be heard, and the occasional sightings of human forms that emerge and then retreat are the only indications left that these people once lived. And they are indications that these people will continue to spend their days on the island of Alcatraz, a place that for many meant no escape.

Rufe McCain

Murdered By a Monster...

Some famous prisoners were unknown during their lifetimes and became famous specifically because of their reported haunting of Alcatraz after their deaths there. Rufe McCain is the most famous of those prisoners...and is, in fact, the most well-known and oft-reported ghost of Alcatraz. McCain was a prisoner who served a good portion of his time in the D Block, the solitary unit cellblock that is said to be the home to most of the spirits that haunt the area. The most haunted of those cells, McCain's, is Cell D14.

"Cell 14 on D block continues to resonate with the sorrow and despair of a criminal who spent three solitary years in the tiny area. Today, no matter how warm the weather, that one cell remains icy cold" (Smith, 2004, p. 174-176). "The temperature inside the cell house can be in the 70s, yet 14D is still cold...so cold that you need a jacket if you spend any time in it" (Taylor, 2006). In particular, there is an icy spot in the corner of the cell and "people who contact this cold spot often feel unsettling emotions" (Dwyer, 2005).

Right: From outside, looking into Cell D14. This is the old cell of Rufe McCain, the ghost who is most often reported by people relating tales of a haunted Alcatraz.

14

1

Who exactly was Rufe McCain and why does he continue to haunt Alcatraz today? Perhaps it is because he himself was haunted during the time he was serving out his sentence in this prison. Reports of ghosts in that cell date back to the time that McCain was a prisoner there. There is one story about the ghost of Rufe McCain that seems to make the rounds of storytellers more often than any of the other versions of the story that have been told. In this story, it is said McCain was locked in a solitary cell and began screaming wildly as soon as the door closed behind him. Through his nearly incoherent screams, he conveyed the message that there was a strange animal with glowing red eyes that was locked in there with him. Of course, no one believed this crazy man who was screaming inside of his cell. He obviously just wanted to be released, didn't he?

Maybe not. As the story goes, McCain kept on screaming for hours and hours. Then he fell silent, deathly silent.

Fatally silent, as it would turn out....

For, when the guards opened the cell door the next day to check on McCain, they discovered him dead in his cell. Around his throat were the marks of his murderer's hands. Some people said that he must have somehow managed to choke himself, but an autopsy showed that this simply wasn't possible. Most medical experts agree that the body's natural reflex to fight for life makes it impossible to strangle yourself in this way. But, McCain was reportedly alone in that cell, so what really happened?

Some people said that a guard who had access to the cell must have choked him. Others said that perhaps the guards let another inmate in to murder him. There was no final answer about this man's death.

But the story doesn't end there....

There were reports that the man was actually seen the next day — in the lineup for count that was done by guards. (Taylor, 2006)

Reports of red, glowing eyes in that cell had been common during the time that the prisoner, who turned out to be inmate McCain, was placed in there...McCain was apparently killed by a ghostly spirit. Many accounts refer to the eyes as belonging to *The Thing*, but some report that they belonged to "the ghostly presence of a man dressed in late 1800s prison attire" (Legends of America, 2003–2007). Whoever — or whatever — they belonged to is believed to have killed Rufe McCain.

The history books tell the story of McCain's death differently of course. After all, history is not going to be written to say that a man died at Alcatraz from an unidentifiable monster or the ghost of a dead prisoner from another era. What the history books will tell you is that McCain was stabbed to death in the industry building by another inmate, Henri Young (GAzis-Sax, 1996). This famous tale was dramatized in a Hollywood movie about Young's life[3]. This movie has been reported to be factually incorrect and may or may not be the actual cause of McCain's death. But that doesn't explain the red, glowing eyes in the corner of D14 today, nor does it explain how McCain's spirit still seems to be present there.

But perhaps what can explain the chill is that it is actually Henri Young continuing to haunt Rufe McCain in that cell. You see, McCain and Young had been having problems for quite some time, ever since the two had been caught together trying to escape. Young blamed McCain for getting them caught. And the day that Young killed McCain, he did so because "he thought the bank robber and killer sneered at him and drew a line across his throat." This caused Young to feel a chill, "as if a cold, calmly snake had been placed next to (his) skin. (His) head was spinning." So perhaps the chill and unsettling feelings that Young felt from McCain's actions are present in McCain's old cell today (GAzis-Sax, 1996).

Tourists visiting Alcatraz today often report that they do indeed feel the chill of the D-Block cells, especially D14 where Rufe McCain was said to have died. If you enter that cell, you may find that you are overwhelmed by unsettling emotions, perhaps the emotions of a terrified inmate trying to escape his untimely death and to understand what could possibly be the source of those glowing eyes. Or maybe what you feel is merely the emotional release of the hundreds of men who must have spent time being scared and alone in that cell.

Maybe the ghost there is the ghost of Rufe McCain. Maybe it is the ghost of the military prisoner who reportedly killed him and then mocked his death by standing in line the next day at count. Maybe it is the ghost of Henri Young, trying desperately to give McCain that same chill he felt before he murdered McCain. Or perhaps it is some other ghost that lingers there in the small space. Do you really want to hang out in there, waiting to find out?

Abie "Butcher" Maldowitz

Avenging His Death to this Day....

The case of Abie "Butcher" Maldowitz is one in which he became more famous after his ghostly presence was discovered than he actually was during the time in which he inhabited Alcatraz as a living, breathing person. He wasn't a prisoner who was known by name in the annals of Alcatraz incarceration history. But he lived and died in the prison at Alcatraz and his name became known when his ghost was discovered there. His spirit was discovered in the deserted laundry room in Cell Block C by medium and psychic Sylvia Browne who was called in to investigate the unusually large amount of ghostly activity reported in the area. (Smith, 2004, p. 174–176)

Reports of who precisely called Browne in to investigate the ghostly activity are varied. Some say that she was "asked by the Park Service to determine what was causing the screams and crying often heard in the dungeon area of Cell Block C" (Dwyer, 2005). Regardless of who asked Browne to investigate or where precisely she did her investigation, the accounts of what she found there are reported to all lead to the story of the life and death of Abie "Butcher" Maldowitz.

Upon entering the area where the activity was taking place, Browne "immediately encountered the unseen presence, as well as strong impressions of violence in the Laundry Room. She described sensing 'a tall man, with a bald head and small bead eyes,' which was later determined to be Butcher, 'a hitman with Murder Incorporated before they caught him'" (Legends of America, 2003-2007). Research into the prison records showed that a fellow inmate murdered Maldowitz in the laundry room. Browne believed that his spirit remained there because of the anger he felt at this unjust death. She tried to help Maldowitz's soul find peace, but he resisted her efforts and continues to haunt the area today (Dwyer, 2005).

Maybe Maldowitz suffered some guilt over the actions he had committed when he was a free man. After all, the Murder Incorporated group was no small deal. As described by Frank Heaney, the youngest guard ever to work at Alcatraz, one of the jobs held by people in this group was to make cement shoes for the corpses of the people that they killed. "They'd prop a body up with its feet in wash pails, fill the pails with cement and let it harden, then dump the corpse off a pier, and that was the end of it — fish food" (Heaney, 1987, p. 91). But it's unlikely.

Today, Butcher can be heard making a ruckus in the entire area that makes up Cell Block C, although he is particularly fond of what used to be the laundry room. Most commonly, what is heard are sounds similar to the physical violence of an altercation. If you were to close your eyes while listening to it, you could imagine bodies being slammed against walls and hear the smacking of flesh against flesh. And... you would eventually hear a gasp for air...followed by silence. But, why would you close your eyes in Alcatraz today? It is much better to do your best to block out the sounds of the past.

Smitty

The Amazing Escape Artist....

...

Smitty was the nickname of a prisoner who was known amongst the guards for his ability to get in and out of anything, no matter how tightly secured it seemed to be. Maybe this is why Smitty ended up at Alcatraz, a place from which there was said to be no escape. Although he didn't escape from the prison itself, Smitty was often getting in and out of different parts of the prison. In fact, he was sometimes called upon by the guards to show off this skill, either for their own amusement or to assist them with something.

In his account about his time as a prison guard at Alcatraz, George Gregory recounts two different occasions on which Smitty showed off this talent of his. In the first case, it started with Smitty trying to play a joke on the officer doing the head count of the prisoners in his cell. When he looked into the treatment unit cell where Smitty was supposed to be located, the officer saw no one. A deeper search of the room found Smitty tied underneath his bed bunk, appearing as though he was hanging himself.

The officer decided to not let this infraction go unpunished and ordered that Smitty be untied and then put into hand restraints so that he couldn't hurt himself. Smitty put up no resistance to being tied into the long gloves that were used at that time to restrict all hand movement. Smitty, with hands gloved, was locked in a hospital cell. "Sure enough, Smitty removed the restraints" (Gregory, 2002, p. 96-97).

On the other occasion described by Gregory, Smitty helped him out with a problem he was having. As he describes it, "I made the mistake of locking my keys in a cabinet. No point in getting excited about it as long as Smitty worked for me. I called him over and asked him to unlock the cabinet door. He wouldn't let me watch, but he opened the cabinet" (Gregory, 2002, p. 96-97).

And perhaps that is why you can sometimes hear someone getting into something in the prison today, but you'll find no one there if you try to inspect the source of the sound. You'll hear doors open and close, but no one will be there. You'll hear keys jangling playfully as though someone has just agreed to get them for you, but is holding them out of your reach before giving them back. He probably doesn't spend all of his time at Alcatraz...why bother when he can escape now through the clouds. But Smitty seems to visit now and then to engage in his hijinks and get the last laugh.

The Naked Nazi

 Sitting Still....

Not many people are aware of the fact, but three Nazi spies were once sentenced to imprisonment at Alcatraz. It was during the late 1940s. As the story goes, years earlier, a U-boat filled with Nazi spies who were escaping Europe landed on the coast of Florida and the spies on the boat dispersed all throughout the United States. This led, of course, to a massive search. Three of the Nazi spies who were ultimately caught were sentenced to Alcatraz (Heaney, 1987, p. 90).

The lives of these spies were relatively quiet as far as life on Alcatraz goes. Although the other inmates were aware of the status of these prisoners, they didn't seem to pay much attention to them at all. Only the oldest of the three even did much interacting with the other inmates and that was limited to the standard politeness between prisoners who are mostly trying to stay out of each other's way (Heaney, 1987, p. 90-91).

One of the three Nazi spies, however, was more problematic than the others. As a result, he ultimately ended up on D-block. "He was pretty nutty; he didn't communicate, went around naked, wouldn't eat, and was skinny as a rail" (Heaney, 1987, p. 90). All of these traits really didn't make him a whole lot different from any of the other inmates who were stuck on D-block. And perhaps that's why you probably couldn't distinguish his spirit there today from the others who seem to spend their time haunting the halls of Alcatraz.

Except for the fact that he's always naked. He consistently refused to wear clothes during the time that he was imprisoned at Alcatraz. Although he didn't die on the island, it's possible that his ghost has returned, because a skinny man in the nude has frequently appeared in ghostly form to visitors of the island. He is usually seen sitting in the front corner of a cell—where his bed would've been during the time that he was incarcerated. He never speaks, just sits there, a human form that is transparent.

The Ghosts Who Go Unnamed

Strange Sounds, Sights, & Sensations...

"Oddly enough it is not just the spirits of the prisoners who died while serving sentences on Alcatraz Island whose souls remain. Some of those who died elsewhere have returned to haunt the place. Most of the hauntings take the form of inexplicable sounds. People frequently hear gruesome, ghostly sounds—men screaming and crying, walking or running through the corridors, whispering to the other souls who were their fellow inmates" (Smith, 2004, p. 174–176). The hauntings are reported by people visiting the island today, but they have been occurring since before Alcatraz was open to the public.

The guards who worked at the federal prison — and their families who lived with them on the island — frequently reported different events that can only be described as a haunting. Strange smells would emanate in various parts of the island and, although people tried to attribute them to odors drifting in with the Bay wind, they seemed to have no definable source. Cold spots located throughout Alcatraz Island were dismissed as being odd pockets of chill created by the unique wind patterns around the island, but many on the island said that the chills they felt couldn't have anything to do with the wind. Furthermore, these guards and their family would heard crying, moaning, and groaning in places where there were no people and some even reported seeing the physical form of someone that could only be a ghost.

The ghost form that was seen most often was that of old soldiers. Gunshots were also heard throughout the island, shots that sounded so realistic that guards would immediately go on the alert, thinking that a prisoner had escaped and somehow gotten hold of a gun (Taylor, 2006). Multiple people would hear the shots, but they wouldn't seem to have any source. Another thing that was regularly spotted was smoke. Guards would actually run to the source of the smoke (often the deserted laundry room), planning to put out a fire, only to find that there was nothing burning there (Taylor, 2006).

"Even Warden Johnston, who did not believe in ghosts, once encountered the unmistakable sound of a person sobbing while he accompanied some guests on a tour of the prison. He swore that the sounds came from inside of the dungeon walls. The strange sounds were followed by an ice-cold wind that swirled through the entire group. He could offer no explanation for the weird events" (Legends of America, 2003–2007). And Johnston wasn't the only person who felt or saw spirits in his home on Alcatraz Island. "Since the 1940s, apparitions have been seen at the site of the now burned-out shell of the warden's house. During a Christmas Party at Warden Johnston's, several guards told the story of a ghostly man who suddenly appeared before them wearing a gray suit, brimmed cap, and sporting mutton-chop sideburns. As the startled guards stared at the apparition, the room suddenly turned very cold and the fire in the Ben Franklin stove was extinguished. Less than a minute later, the spirit vanished."

Guards and inmates alike reported possible ghosts all throughout the island of Alcatraz...ghosts who were said to be the spirits of the Confederate soldiers who lost their freedom (and for some, their lives) on the island. These spirits showed up in prisoner counts, especially out in the exercise yard. They stirred up activity in The Sally Port. They filled the laundry room with smoke. And they turned on radios in Building 64.

Some of the spirits that are reportedly sensed by visitors to Alcatraz today are likely to be the same spirits that haunted the guards who worked at Alcatraz. Others are surely the spirits of the inmates who lived and died during the time that Alcatraz was a working prison. The prison hospital is surely one spot where the strange sounds are likely to be coming from an old inmate. In fact, it's possible that at least one of the inmates haunting the hospital can be identified, although not be named.

The hospital is closed to the public on tour of Alcatraz so not many have heard the sounds that come from this location, but there are frequent reports of activity taking place up there. Often, security crewmembers will make their way there to check out the source of the commotion only to find that there's no one (visibly) there. And often, if they stand there for a moment, head cocked and ears perked to try and identify the source of the sound, they'll hear whispers. It has been reported that, "I feel good," is a quiet statement that reverberates throughout the walls of the hospital.

The statement doesn't make sense if you don't know some of the history behind it. After all, who feels good at Alcatraz? Especially in the hospital. But there was indeed a convict who uttered those words as his very last. George Gregory relates the tale of this man in his memoir. He writes, "Entering the cell, I pulled off the blanket — what a mess! The convict had picked at the veins in his wrists until he was well on the way to bleeding to death ... We got the convict to the hospital as quickly as we could, (but) it was too late. He had lost too much blood and his veins had collapsed. According to the other convicts in the hospital that night, just a minute or so before the end he sat up in bed and said, "I feel good," then laid back and died" (Gregory, 2002, p. 102).

This inmate may be heard sometimes continuing to gasp his last breath in the old prison hospital. But the place is filled with spirits, so he is probably not alone. And he has plenty of company throughout the rest of the building by ghosts who go unnamed in the annals of history. One of these ghosts seems to be stuck on Cell Block A where he can be heard screaming loudly every now and then. Many more continue to make catcalls and whistles at the now-invisible "fresh fish" walking between the cellblocks on Broadway. And at least one or two hang around in the cafeteria and the library, making a little bit of noise and causing distinctly unsettling feelings for some of the tourists who take the time to turn off their audio tapes and notice what is happening around them.

These ghosts may not belong to men whose names are known. Perhaps this is part of the problem; they spent so long being "just a number" that they don't know themselves well enough to figure out where they're supposed to go now that their lives at Alcatraz have ended. But they remain on the island still. No one can say how many of them there are. Surely, some remain from the long ago days of the federal prison at Alcatraz. And most of them are definitely the inmates who were housed alongside the more famous criminals who also haunt the halls.

But are inmates and soldiers the only ones to haunt the island? Besides the famous case of Mr. Cline's and the bloody hand marks on the wall, are there any guards whose spirits continue to pace the nighttime halls of Alcatraz? Did any of the wives and children who lived there with those guards find it to be a place to return to after their passing? And what of the little Native American girl who has been reported as being seen in the old prison mortuary? Who is she and will she ever be able to move on?

Part IV:

People Are Talking

What the Experts Say

Psychics, Researchers, and Writers

Where there are ghosts, there are experts who want to find out more about these ghosts. Psychics and mediums, like the well-known (primarily for her appearances on "The Montel Williams" show) psychic Sylvia Browne, have been called to Alcatraz to uncover the source of disturbing sounds and feelings on the island. Paranormal research groups have gained permission to access the island at night with their equipment in order to record and photograph the sounds and sights that can't always be captured by the human senses. And authors and other professional researchers have searched high and low for answers to the questions that numerous Alcatraz visitors have had about their experiences on the island.

Psychics and Mediums

There are a number of psychics and mediums who are known for their work in the Bay Area. San Francisco itself is filled with ghosts and the surrounding regions from the East Bay to the southern and northern regions of the Pacific Coast have had their share of disturbing history and reported spirit activity. But there is a particular appeal for visiting Alcatraz, to help sort out the facts from the fiction as much as possible.

Yet, not too many psychics have reported on their findings at Alcatraz.

"Numerous psychics have reported cold spots, harsh and sudden emotional bursts, apparitions claiming abuse, vibrations and a myriad of other ghostly traces" (Alcatraz Hauntings, 2007). However, the records of these reports are mostly lost to time.

One psychic does stand out—Sylvia Browne. Best known for her regular appearances on "The Montel Williams" show, Browne is a psychic with a lifetime of experience in communicating with spirits. She discovered her talents in this area when she was a mere three months old, and has devoted her life to using these talents to assist others in finding peace with the spirits in their lives (Browne, 2006). Because of her history in working with spirits in the San Francisco Bay Area and the credibility she had gained over the years, Browne was called in by the Park Service to assess the situation regarding the events that led to her discovery of the ghost that was determined to be Abie "Butcher" Maldowitz.

Although Browne is the most well-known psychic to have visited the island, she is not the only one of note. Psychic Carla Baron also visited Alcatraz back in 2004. Baron is a nationally-known psychic who has used her gifts to work in conjunction with the FBI and other crime fighting agencies. She is most known for her appearances on the Court TV show "Psychic Detectives" and the British Program "Dead Famous" (Baron, 2007).

Working in conjunction with "Dead Famous" and a film company called TwoFour Productions, she was called in to investigate Alcatraz. With her were a "sensitive" named Chris Fleming and a ghost-hunter by the name of Richard Senate. Reportedly, "Senate locked himself in cell 12-D, where an evil spirit is said to make his home. As the steel door was closed, the ghost-hunter felt icy fingers wrap around his neck, while the psychic experienced visions of the bodies of twisted and dismembered men" (Ghost Trackers, 2004).

Maybe it was just his imagination getting a hold of him. But...maybe not.

Paranormal Researchers

While psychics tend to be the ones with the most credibility in terms of their ghost hunting expertise and their ability to both discern the activities that once took place and their knowledge of how to communicate with the dead, they are not the professionals who are most intimately experienced with finding ghost activity. Instead, this task frequently falls to the skills of paranormal researchers. These groups of people are particularly useful to the history of ghosts on Alcatraz because of the difficulty of discerning the rumors from the potential facts on this island.

All of the rumors surrounding the famous lives and deaths of the infamous men who lived here, the cacophony of tourists circulating all throughout the island, and the shrieking of the birds overhead combined together to create a noise, both internal and external, over which it is impossible to hear. It can be difficult to be sure that the sounds you think you can notice are really there, despite that they would be easily recognizable as ghost activity in any other setting. Sure, you hear screams, but they could be the joking cries of a group of kids visiting the island on vacation. And yes, you feel the strange icy chill down your spine when you enter certain areas of the island, but that can be easily attributed to the chill of the wind that always permeates the Bay Area.

It is the job of paranormal researchers to sort the every day from the out-of-place, to determine which activities and actions on an island are ghost activity and which are merely the every day strangeness of a place with a history as odd as that of Alcatraz. And so, paranormal researchers from all around California—and even from other parts of the country—have come to Alcatraz together to see what they can find.

On a 2003 tour of Alcatraz, researchers from the American Paranormal group confirmed reported ghost activity near the cell of Al Capone. Capturing two orbs in photographs taken in the area, these researchers were able to say that the rumors that Capone (or someone anyway) was still in the area were more than likely to be true. But perhaps of more interest on that tour was the findings of the group in the area of the old hospital ward. The conference attendees experienced "thick, harsh feelings. Many of them also were 'seeing' floating lights as well as a few 'seeing' apparitions" (American Paranormal Investigators, 2003).

Other paranormal researchers have not had as much luck confirming or negating the presence of ghost activity on the island. For example, a trip by the Paranormal Activity Investigators found nothing new in addition to the material with which they were already familiar, but did report being strangely unable to work their cameras during their trip (Patrick, 2005). This wasn't the only time that a paranormal research group failed to capture pictures at the island because of an unexplainable camera malfunction. In 2004, the San Diego paranormal research project reported: "Laura from Chicago reports on her experience of cold spots in Cell Block D ... hair on the backs of necks stood up, tried to take pictures but the camera wouldn't work even though it worked everywhere else" (Laura, 2004).

The lack of clarity that paranormal research groups have been able to provide regarding the ghost activity of Alcatraz only serves to further exacerbate the difficulty of discerning fact from fiction when it comes to the history of Alcatraz and the spirits that may or may not be there today. But the work that these groups have contributed is invaluable, as they have used their tools to add to the stories that are coming out of the prison even to this day.

The author behind the bars of a cell at Alcatraz. Has she seen a ghost? She'll never tell.

The Dirt Dug Up By Research

Psychics and paranormal researchers are not the only professionals who come to check out the island. In fact, they aren't even the most common ones who head there. Instead, this category falls to authors and other creative researchers. This makes sense. In a place where so much rich history has occurred and where there is such a blurring between fact and fiction, there is a well of possibility for the storyteller. And of course, to tell the story, one must know it.

One of the things that an author has to do when researching material for a book is to become intimately familiar with the subject of the book. Anyone who is going to be writing about the history of ghosts at Alcatraz, then, is required to go spend time at Alcatraz, seeking out ghostly experiences of his or her own. And for many, the experiences are so frightening that the research trip to the area is the last one that they'll willingly take there.

Two sets of authors who have written about the ghosts of Alcatraz reported feeling the negative energy often associated with Cell 14D (the old cell of Rufe McCain). In one case, the co-authors of *Haunted Houses* (Richard Winter and Nancy Osborn) reported that they, along with a park ranger who was acting as their guide, "felt strong vibrations and tingling sensations in their hands and arms. Convinced that something or someone was there with them, Osborn stated that she had never felt so much psychic energy in one spot" (Legends of America, 2003–2007).

Similarly, when visiting Alcatraz for his research in co-authoring *Haunted Alcatraz*, Michael Kouri felt tingling sensations in the same cell. Additionally, "he also tells of 'seeing' a small man with his head shaved who 'told' of being beaten" (Legends of America, 2003–2007). Kouri is familiar with such experiences because of his work and research as the author of numerous books on ghosts in various areas (Kouri, 2007).

Of course, it is not only authors who have to do their research on the island to complete their creative works. "In 1992, Alcatraz was featured on the popular television program "Sightings," where several of the Park Service staff confirmed the haunted history of the prison. Among the stories told by staff were unexplainable crashing sounds, running footsteps, unearthly screams, cell doors that mysteriously closed of their own accord, moans, chains rattling, and the constant feelings of being watched. "Sightings" also enlisted the help of psychic investigator,

Peter James, to get his impressions as he walked through the prison. James soon described hearing the voices of men who had been driven mad, and experiences of abuse, fear and pain" (Legends of America, 2003–2007).

These are just a few of the creative people who have visited the island of Alcatraz for research and experienced things that they didn't expect to experience. As for your author, she did her research and visited Alcatraz more than once, but her lips are sealed as to whether or not she experienced any ghostly activity during her explorations of the island. After all, she wouldn't want to scare you.

What Others Have Said

"As the years have passed, ghost hunters, authors, crime buffs, and curiosity-seekers have visited the island and many of them have left with feelings of strangeness. Perhaps those who experience the "ghostly side" of Alcatraz most often are the National Park Service employees who sometimes spend many hours here alone. For the most part, the rangers claim to not believe in the supernatural, but occasionally, one of them will admit that weird things happen here that they cannot explain" (Taylor, 2006).

The point here is that it is not just professionals and people with a vested interest in finding spirits in the area who have reported ghost activity on Alcatraz. Sure, one would expect séances to turn up ghosts and authors trying to find ghosts on Alcatraz to report sensing them there, but when the average person who works on the island or visits there also sees ghosts activity, then it is likely that something spooky really is going on.

Many different individuals have recounted their experiences with ghostly activity on the island. Most of these people have similar stories. From a trip to the island in 2001, Michael Snyder reports a tale that is common to many of the visitors of Alcatraz:

"There is a part in the tour where the audio tape tells you to enter into a cell, and because of its proximity to where I was at the time of the tape's instruction, I entered into 13D. At that point an "inmate" began to talk on the tape about how dark it was in there, and how he used to stay busy by tossing a button around in the cell and trying to find it. He also had hallucinations in the dark. He claimed he could focus on a tiny light in his mind until it grew brighter and eventually he could be watching a TV show in there. At this point, the narrator said to turn the tape off and close your eyes to see the light he was talking about. THAT was when I noticed something out of the ordinary. Up until that point we were in the midst of a pretty big crowd. At that moment, the crowd had moved on and I was alone inside of Cell 13D, and my wife was outside waiting for me. As I closed my eyes I noticed a feeling come over me like I was losing my equilibrium. I also started to feel a little nauseous. I'm not claustrophobic, but I was beginning to feel very uneasy and claustrophobic in that cell. I had had some experiences with spiritual presences as a teenager, so I immediately suspected that these feelings I was getting were caused by something supernatural. I walked out of the cell and asked my wife to go in there with me. I told her I felt weird in there and asked her to close her eyes and tell me what she felt. She agreed, and came inside the cell with me. After a brief period of time, she told me that she didn't feel good at all. She was feeling dizzy and sick to her stomach. I was amazed that she had the same feelings I did even though I didn't tell her how I felt. This confirmed my suspicions of a presence in there, so I told her that I felt that something very terrible had happened in that cell. Perhaps someone had been tortured or murdered in that cell. I wondered if that person's tortured spirit was still in the cell. Out of curiosity we also went into 12D and 14D. Neither one felt as bad to us as 13D, although 12 seemed a little worse than 14. After this experience my wife told me she had also felt uneasy in most of the rest of Alcatraz, but especially in the kitchen and the library. (Snyder, 2006)

Left: **The library of Alcatraz.**

Plenty of other people in addition to Michael Snyder have helped to confirm ghost stories on the island. Even people who "don't believe in ghosts" frequently report odd occurrences during their visit to Alcatraz. For example, from "The Real Haunts" user forum on Alcatraz comes a report of someone who visited Alcatraz a few years back with a nephew. The two of them "have no interest in or even like the subject of ghosts," finding it to be "kinda boring to be honest." And true enough; their experience actually on the island was fun, but not spooky. That is...until they got home.

The traveler had snapped some pictures in the darkness of the solitary confinement cells. She reports: "Later when we were looking over the pictures, we were very surprised to find a man or who we thought was a fellow tourist standing in the cell." Recollecting taking the picture, the traveler did not remember anyone being in the cell with her at the time. However, she discounted the experience and was well on her way to forgetting it when her nephew insisted on sending it to a photography lab to get it checked out. She says that the lab was "very intrigued" and, although she won't say for sure that she believes in ghosts, she isn't denying that something strange happened since she's sure that no one was in the cell with her when the picture was taken (Betty, 2006).

These travelers are hardly the only ones to have had strange experiences happen, including those associated with developing their pictures. One couple reports that on a trip they took to Alcatraz in June 2005, they were visiting during the last tour of the day, which is known as the Night Tour. They said: "We specifically purchased two disposable cameras so we could feel free to take individual, random pictures as we went along." Nothing odd yet, but almost as soon as they arrived, the couple felt inexplicable changes in their moods, getting angry and irritated at each other for no reason, a situation which is not common to them. This situation made them decide to separate during their self-guided tour (Norma, 2006).

Again, nothing particularly frightening happened during their tour of Alcatraz. They went along, feeling a little sense of eeriness but no real fear. Then they met back up and continued their visit to the San Francisco Bay Area. Upon returning home, the wife took her camera in to get it developed. She didn't see anything "ghostly," but what she did see was a photograph of herself, taken from outside the bars of the cell, wearing an expression as though something has caught her off guard. What is strange about this is that she was in possession of her camera the entire time and didn't ask anyone to take a photograph of her. Of course, she thought that was weird, but almost dismissed it, figuring that somehow she had forgotten that she let her picture be taken (Norma, 2006).

However, when her husband's camera was developed about a week later, there was a similar picture on it. The photograph is of the husband with his back turned to the camera. Curious about the situation, the couple checked the negatives for each camera. On each set of negatives, there is a black, blank image where the photos of the two of them appear. They could never explain how this happened, and although they don't believe in ghosts, they agree that they have no other way to define this experience (Norma, 2006).

So, professionals, quasi-professionals, ghost-lovers, and those who "don't believe in ghosts" all agree that there is something going on at Alcatraz that simply cannot be explained by anything other than spirit activity.

Part V

Your Trip to Alcatraz

The What, When, & How

Perhaps these tales of ghosts on Alcatraz has piqued your interest and you want to go check it out for yourself. Before you do, make sure to do your research and your preparation. While a trip to Alcatraz is generally safe — after all, thousands of tourists do it each year — it is always wise to take some extra precautions when ghost-hunting is on your agenda.

One thing to keep in mind is that, whether or not you experience any ghosts, you should prepare emotionally for the possibility that you might come into contact with them. It is better to be prepared and err on the side of caution than to not be prepared. In addition to your emotional preparation, you should do some physical preparation for your trip. Be sure to double check that all of the ghost-hunting materials you intend to bring to Alcatraz are allowed on the island *(see the Glossary at the end of this book for additional information)*.

Finally, do your research into the history of the hauntings of Alcatraz in advance so that you know what you are looking for. After all, there are going to be dozens, if not hundreds, of other people around you and it is easy to lose your focus. Be aware of the history of the island, other reports of hauntings, and the locations of the areas you wish to focus on.

Despite doing this research, you should go to the island with an open mind. Just because others have seen certain ghosts in certain areas doesn't mean that you will experience these same spirits. And just because certain areas of Alcatraz aren't yet reported to have ghost hauntings doesn't mean that it's impossible for you to experience them. "Proper preparation and an ability to mentally block out the modern world can help the visitor hear screams and cries of the dead on Alcatraz Island" (Dwyer, 2005).

Ultimately, Alcatraz is a spooky place. Its history makes it so and its location in the bay does nothing to diminish its eeriness. Whether or not you directly experience ghost activity during your trip to Alcatraz, you will almost undoubtedly find that your trip there was well worth taking.

The Emotional Preparation

You may scoff at the idea that you need to emotionally prepare for a trip to Alcatraz. After all, hundreds and thousands of people take the tour of Alcatraz every year and there are hardly support groups out there for survivors of the trek. But if you are planning to go to Alcatraz with an eye towards looking out for ghosts, you're going to want to be more emotionally prepared than most. Perhaps you won't experience anything unsettling and you won't need anyone to help you work through it later, but, as they say, it's always better to be safe than sorry. And the emotional preparation that you do for your ghost-hunting trip to Alcatraz will probably be good for you anyway.

There are two different emotional levels on which you will want to prepare for your ghost-hunting expedition to Alcatraz. First, you will want to work on the internal emotional aspects of the experience. And secondly, you will want to find an external support network to assist you in psychologically handling the experience. I know, it sounds like a bit much for just going to see some old dilapidated prison cells, but you'll be glad that you did it if you do start experiencing any sort of confusing emotions after the trip. And besides, the people who form your external support network could be great people to have around irrelevant of their emotional support.

Doing the internal emotional preparation for a ghost-hunting trip to Alcatraz really just means spending some time with yourself. Often, our lives are so busy as we jump from project to project that we really don't take the time to process things as much as we ought to. When we fail to properly pay attention to what's going on inside of ourselves, we often end up having to deal with the effects after the fact. Don't let that happen to you in regards to your Alcatraz trip. Instead, sit down with yourself and check in for a moment.

This doesn't need to be some formal process. The goal is merely to find out what your interest in ghosts is, how much experience you feel you have with it, and what kind of emotional repercussions and exploration of that interest might have for you. For example, perhaps your interest in ghosts of Alcatraz has to do with the fact that you want to write a research paper about it. Let's say that the topic interests you on an intellectual level, but you aren't actually very experienced in the topic. You figure that you'll go to Alcatraz, ask a few questions, see nothing unusual, and leave to write your paper. But what if, while you're there, you do experience some ghostly phenomenon? Are you going to be prepared to deal with it?

By asking yourself what your intentions are and how well you will cope with the "what if" of a situation that may arise, you let your mind begin to work out the details of the situation. This in and of itself is great emotional preparation for the trip. By knowing what you would do if you encountered the unexpected, you have made yourself identify your coping mechanisms. You can get to these answers by journaling about them, by meditating, or just by taking time to think them through during the course of the days leading up to your trip.

But you should also identify where you might be able to go in order to get additional answers to any questions that come up for you. That gets us to the second part of your emotional preparation: the establishment of a support network. In reality, you probably already have one. You have a spouse or a best friend or a sibling who will be there for you if things go awry. But you should think carefully about whom in your life you would share your issues with if any come up during the ghost-hunting expedition. After all, it's great that your wife is there for you, but is she going to take you seriously when you say that you felt a ghost? You need to make sure that you have at least one person in your life that will be non-judgmental about whatever experiences you may or may not have during your trip to Alcatraz.

The other part of the external support network comes from finding a person or group who is already somewhat familiar with the ghostly experiences of Alcatraz. These people will be more likely to take you seriously, but just as important, they will be able to provide you with resources for answering any questions that might come up for you. In general, for this type of external support network, you will be looking to find a local ghost-hunter or even an online paranormal research group.

If you find someone locally, make sure that you make contact prior to your trip to Alcatraz. After all, there's no guarantee that that the guy who leads the ghost tours in your city is going to have any interest in having a conversation with you, let alone being there for you if things get weird. Don't lose heart if the professionals that you contact aren't interested in your story. That's why you're doing this emotional work beforehand, rather than after the fact. You're working to find the people that are interested enough in your experience to be there for you no matter what happens. You'll know these people when you find them, because you'll be eager to meet with them after your Alcatraz trip, whether it's for that needed emotional support or simply to share your experiences over coffee at the corner café.

Rather than finding someone local to function as your quasi-professional emotional support (or in addition to finding that person), you should strongly consider using the Internet resources that are available. Paranormal research groups and websites related to studies of ghosts frequently have user forums that you can join. On these forums, you will find people who have had experiences similar to yours and you'll be able to discuss those experiences with them. Other people often act as the best resource for finding tools for better understanding ghost experiences so you should do what you can to find them.

The reality is that you probably aren't going to experience anything so awful at Alcatraz that you are going to need extensive internal resources and a support network to assist you in coping with it. But the other part of that reality is the *"what if?"* If you really do plan on finding out the truth (or at least your truth) about ghosts at Alcatraz, you should prepare for the experience. That way, there are no surprises. Or at least, there are none that you can't deal with.

The Physical Preparation

Once you've done the hard part of emotionally preparing for your trip to Alcatraz, you're ready to do the physical preparation. This means that you will want to gather together all of the ghost-hunting materials that you plan to take to Alcatraz. You will also want to do your background research into the history of the ghosts of Alcatraz (which you've clearly already started since you're reading this far into the book). And finally, you will want to plan your trip and book your tickets.

But first thing's first, you need some ghost-hunting tools. You probably don't to want to get too fancy or invest too much money in this area and that's okay, because it really isn't necessary. If you do plan on being more than just a one-time ghost researcher, you might invest in certain advanced equipment *(see the Glossary at the end of this book for more information)*. But for just basic ghost hunting at Alcatraz, there are only a few things that you'll need.

You'll want to get a camera that you can use to take photographs inside and outside of Alcatraz. Frequently, the ghostly experiences that are had on Alcatraz come in the form of human shapes seen on film or digital camera screens after the trip has ended. So, you'll want to take plenty of pictures. Whether you use film or digital depends on your own preferences since they both have their benefits. A film camera is more likely to capture objects that you don't see when you're in the cell house and on the grounds of Alcatraz. The surprise of developing the film and finding figures there that weren't with you on the trip (and which might not even be on the negatives) is a frightening experience indeed. On the other hand, digital cameras often have video recording capability that can better capture movement of the shadows that might appear during your explorations.

So either a film or a digital camera will do for your photography at Alcatraz. Or, of course, you could always take both. The one thing to keep in mind is that you don't want to get a brand new, fancy camera right before your trip. You want something that you're comfortable using. You're not trying to create fine art or capture the great light of Alcatraz (although it's certainly a place where striking photographs can be taken). You're there to see what you can get on film that you didn't see with your eyes.

In addition to some sort of camera, you will probably want to bring some audio equipment with you. This is because there are a great number of sounds on Alcatraz. The shrieking of the birds overhead, the laughter and chatter of the other tourists, and the lectures from tour guides will consistently distract you throughout your tour. By taking an audio recording of your Alcatraz experience, you will have the ability later to go back and listen to all of the sounds that you were too distracted to hear when you were on the island. You can return home later and listen carefully to what is on the tape, and perhaps it is at this time that you will be able to identify the birdcalls of Robert "Birdman" Stroud or the soft sobbing of the little Native American girl in the mortuary.

Additionally, having camera and audio equipment will help you to relax. This is because you will know that you'll be able to look and listen more carefully later. This gives you the opportunity to pay more attention to the sensory experience that you will be having at Alcatraz. And this is when you will be able to tell if you can feel icy fingers on the back of your neck or if you are overwhelmed with unsettling emotions in certain rooms. Having the right equipment allows you to have the right experience.

But gathering the right equipment is only part of your physical preparation. Just as important is your research into the existing history of ghosts at Alcatraz. You should know what has been experienced in the prison before you so that you can keep an eye out for it. Do all of the research that you can, including becoming familiar with a map of the haunted locations at the prison. Learn about the ghosts and then learn about the general history of the area, from all of its various time periods. The more that you know going in, the more that you will take out of your Alcatraz experience—whether or not you experience any ghosts.

The Best Time to Go

With the right frame of mind, the right tools, and research, you are ready to book your trip to Alcatraz. Alcatraz is open almost every single day of the year and you usually only need to get tickets a few days in advance, so it should be fairly easy to book your ferry ride and tour

Be careful when getting back on the boat after a ghost-hunting tour at Alcatraz. After all, you wouldn't want to help someone who is still stuck there escape.

of the island. But to get the most out of your ghost-hunting experience, there are a few things that you'll want to keep in mind. For example, you'll want to think about the time of day that you'd like to be at Alcatraz and the season during which you would like to take your trip.

Many amateur ghost-hunters are interested in visiting Alcatraz at night. Perhaps this is because we associate ghosts with being scary creatures of the dark. Unfortunately there are no overnight tours of Alcatraz, so that won't be an option for you. But what is an option is that you can take the last tour of the day, which is known as *The Alcatraz Night Tour*. This tour really isn't that late at night so you're not going to get the eerie experience of being at Alcatraz after dark. And you might feel rushed since you won't have as much time to explore as if you had gone earlier in the day. But there will be less people on the island at this time and there will be that night chill in the air so you might find that this is indeed conducive to a good ghost-hunting experience.

Alternatively, you might want to book yourself on the first tour of the day. In comparison with the tours that happen later in the day, there will still be less people at the island. Additionally, you will have the entire day to explore Alcatraz, so you won't be pressured by time. You will have the luxury of being able to sit quietly in a place for a long period of time, observing the sights and sounds in the lulls between high tourist traffic.

To get the most of your ghost-hunting tour, you will probably want to go when there are less travelers there. It's always a busy place, but there are seasons that are better than others for experiencing less people with you on the island. The summertime is, of course, the time when most people are on vacation. They head to San Francisco and they take the tour of Alcatraz when they are there. So it makes sense to avoid the summer season if your schedule gives you that luxury. There is also a burst of activity around the winter holidays. The best time to go is if you can schedule your trip in the weeks just before the Christmas holidays, just before the school year ends (in early May), or just after the school year starts (in mid-September). And you'll want to go on a weekday, instead of a weekend, of course.

But, there isn't ever a really bad time to go to Alcatraz. If you can't go at one of these optimum times, go anyway. Even a weekend afternoon in the middle of summer will give you a chance to see and explore the island and experience Alcatraz for yourself. Do your emotional preparation, bring the tools that you want to have with you, and enjoy the trip. Just watch out for that shadow that might slip onto the boat with you. You don't want to let anyone escape.

Conclusion

The history of Alcatraz is rich and interesting and it can't ever be entirely understood without a trip to the island. Even locals living in the Bay Area — people who often avoid trips to tourist destinations — admit that a visit to Alcatraz is an experience unlike any other. So, even if you don't believe in the history of the hauntings said to populate this spooky place, it is worth your time to go check out the attraction for yourself.

If you go with an open mind, you might find that there is more to Alcatraz than your eyes can see. Whether you go with a mind on ghosts or merely an interest in learning more about the island from a first-hand view, there is bound to be a new dimension added to your Alcatraz knowledge base when you've experienced a trip there for yourself.

Inevitably, when people find out about the research I did in order to be able to write this book with any degree of accuracy, they want to know if I experienced any ghosts on the island myself. I have thought about sharing this story. But I think it's a tale better left untold. Because the thing about Alcatraz is that there is no real truth about this island. It's all subjective...it's all layered. No matter what I do or do not tell you about my trip to the island, Alcatraz will forever remain a place that exists only in shades of grey.

But what I will say is that I live in San Francisco and, while many people who live here never bother to go to Alcatraz because it is considered to be "just for tourists," I highly recommend a trip there to everyone at some point during their stay in the Bay Area. When you stand on that island, surrounded by the icy, choppy waters of the bay and the shrieking cries of the seagulls, you will feel something that you have not felt anywhere else on the planet.

In many ways, Alcatraz itself is a ghost. It is the spirit of a place that it once was. And instead of it visiting you against your will, you go to visit it in order to add a new experience to your lifetime. If you go with this in mind, you *WON'T* be disappointed.

Right: For some people, Alcatraz was a very *DEAD END*.

Glossary

* The following section is provided by the Chester County Paranormal Research Society in Pennsylvania and appears in training materials for new investigators. Please visit www.ChesterCountyprs. com for more information.

Air Probe Thermometer
A thermometer with an external probe that is capable of taking instant measurements of the air temperature.

Anomalous field
A field that cannot be explained or ruled out by various possibilities, and that can be a representation of spirit or paranormal energy present.

Apparition
A transparent form of a human or animal; a spirit.

Artificial field
A field that is caused by electrical outlets, appliances, etc.

Aural Enhancer
A listening device that enhances or amplifies audio signals. i.e., Orbitor Bionic Ear.

Automatic writing
The act of a spirit guiding a human agent in writing a message that is brought through by the spirit.

Base readings
The readings taken at the start of an investigation and are used as a means of comparing other readings taken later during the course of the investigation.

Demonic Haunting
A haunting that is caused by an inhuman or subhuman energy or spirit.

Dowsing Rods
A pair of L-shaped rods or a single Y-shaped rod, used to detect the presence of what the person using them is trying to find.

Electro-static generator
A device that electrically charges the air often used in paranormal investigations/research as a means to contribute to the materialization of paranormal or spiritual energy.

ELF
Extremely Low Frequency.

ELF Meter/EMF Meter
A device that measures electric and magnetic fields.

EMF
Electro Magnetic Field.

EVP
Electronic Voice Phenomena.

False positive
Something that is being interpreted as paranormal within a picture or video and is, in fact, a natural occurrence or defect of the equipment used.

Gamera

A 35mm film camera connected with a motion detector that is housed in a weatherproof container and takes a picture when movement is detected. Made by Silver Creek Industries.

Geiger Counter

A device that measures gamma and x-ray radiation.

Infra Red

An invisible band of radiation at the lower end of the visible light spectrum. With wavelengths from 750 nm to 1 mm, infrared starts at the end of the microwave spectrum and ends at the beginning of visible light. Infrared transmission typically requires an unobstructed line of sight between transmitter and receiver. Widely used in most audio and video remote controls, infrared transmission is also used for wireless connections between computer devices and a variety of detectors.

Intelligent haunting

A haunting of a spirit or other entity that has the ability to interact with the living and do things that can make its presence known.

Milli-gauss

Unit of measurement, measures in 1000th of a gauss and is named for the famous German mathematician, Karl Gauss.

Orbs

Anomalous spherical shapes that appear on video and still photography.

Pendulum

A pointed item that is hung on the end of a string or chain and is used as a means of contacting spirits. An individual will hold the item and let it hang from the fingertips. The individual will ask questions aloud and the pendulum answers by moving.

Poltergeist haunting

A haunting that has two sides, but same kinds of activity in common. Violent outbursts of activity with doors and windows slamming shut, items being thrown across a room and things being knocked off of surfaces. Poltergeist hauntings are usually focused around a specific individual who resides or works at the location of the activity reported, and, in some cases, when the person is not present at the location, activity does not occur. A poltergeist haunting may be the cause of a human agent or spirit/energy that may be present at the location.

Portal

An opening in the realm of the paranormal that is a gateway between one dimension and the next. A passageway for spirits to come and go through. See also Vortex.

Residual haunting

A haunting that is an imprint of an event or person that plays itself out like a loop until the energy that causes it has burned itself out.

Scrying

The act of eliciting information with the use of a pendulum from spirits.

Table Tipping

A form of spirit communication, the act of a table being used as a form of contact. Individuals will sit around a table and lightly place their fingertips on the edge of the table and elicit contact with a spirit. The Spirit will respond by "tipping" or moving the table.

Talking Boards

A board used as a means of communicating with a spirit. Also known as an Ouija Board.

Vortex

A place or situation regarded as drawing into its center all that surrounds it.

White Noise

A random noise signal that has the same sound energy level at all frequencies.

Equipment Explanations

In this section, the Chester County Paranormal Research Society looks at the application and benefits of equipment used on investigations with greater detail. The equipment used for an investigation plays a vital role in the ability to collect objective evidence and helps to determine what is and is not paranormal activity. But a key point to be made here is: the investigator is the most important tool on any investigation. With that said, let us now take a look at the main pieces of equipment used during an investigation...

The Geiger Counter

The Geiger counter is device that measures radiation. A "Geiger counter" usually contains a metal tube with a thin metal wire along its middle. The space in between them is sealed off and filled with a suitable gas and with the wire at about +1000 volts relative to the tube.

An ion or electron penetrating the tube (or an electron knocked out of the wall by X-rays or gamma rays) tears electrons off atoms in the gas. Because of the high positive voltage of the central wire, those electrons are then attracted to it. They gain energy that collide with atoms and release more electrons, until the process snowballs into an "avalanche," producing an easily detectable pulse of current. With a suitable filling gas, the flow of electricity stops by itself, or else the electrical circuitry can help stop it.

The instrument was called a "counter" because every particle passing it produced an identical pulse, allowing particles to be counted, usually electronically. But it did not tell anything about their identity or energy, except that they must have sufficient energy to penetrate the walls of the counter.

The Geiger counter is used in paranormal research to measure the background radiation at a location. The working theory in this field is that paranormal activity can effect the background radiation. In some cases, it will increase the radiation levels and in other cases it will decrease the levels.

Digital and 35mm Film Cameras

The camera is an imperative piece of equipment that enabled us to gather objective evidence during a case. Some of the best evidence presented from cases of paranormal activity over the years has been because of photographs taken. If you own your own digital camera or 35mm film camera, you need to be fully aware of what the cameras abilities and limitations are. Digital cameras have been at the center of great debate in the field of paranormal research over the years.

The earlier incarnations of digital cameras were full of inherent problems and notorious for creating "false positive" pictures. A "false positive" picture is a picture that has anomalous elements within the picture that are the result of a camera defect or other natural occurrence. There are many pictures scattered about the Internet that claim to be of true paranormal activity, but in fact they are "false positives." Orbs, defined as anomalous paranormal energy that can show up as balls of light or streaks in still photography or video, are the most controversial pictures of paranormal energy in the field. There are so many theories (good and bad) about the origin of orbs and what they are. Pictures in the CCPRS collection that has an orb—or orbs—are not presented in a way that states that they are absolutely paranormal of nature. I have yet to capture an orb photo that made me feel certain that in fact it is of a paranormal nature.

If you use your own camera, understand that your camera is vital. I encourage all members who own their own cameras to do research on the make and model of the camera and see what other consumers are saying about them. Does the manufacturer give any info regarding possible defects or design flaws with that particular model? Understanding your camera will help to rule out the possibility of interpreting a "false positive" for an authentic picture of paranormal activity.

Video Cameras

The video camera is also a fundamental tool in the investigation as another way for collecting objective evidence that can support the proof of paranormal activity. The video camera can be used in various ways during the investigation. It can be set on a tripod and left in a location where paranormal activity has been reported. It can also be used as a hand-held camera and the investigator will take it with them during their walk through investigation as a means of documenting to hopefully capture anomalous activity on tape. Infra-Red technology has become a feature on most consumer level video cameras and depending on the manufacturer can be called "night shot" or "night alive." What this technology does is allow us to use the camera in zero light. Most cameras with this feature will add a green tint or haze to the camera when it is being used in this mode. A video camera with this ability holds great appeal to the paranormal investigator.

EMF/ELF Meters

EMF=Electro Magnetic Frequency

ELF=Extremely Low Frequency

What is an EMF/ELF meter? Good question. The EMF/ELF meter is a meter that measures Electric and Magnetic fields in an AC or DC current field. It measures in a unit of measurement called "milli-gauss," named for the famous German mathematician, Karl Gauss. Most meters will measure in a range of 1-5 or 1-10 milli-gauss. The reason that EMF meters are used in paranormal research is because of the theory that a spirit or paranormal energy can add to the energy field when it is materializing or is present in a location. The theory says that, typically, an energy that measures between 3-7 milli-gauss may be of a paranormal origin. This doesn't mean that an artificial field can't also measure within this range. That is why we take base readings and make maps notating where artificial fields occur. The artificial fields are a direct result of electricity, i.e. wiring, appliances, light switches, electrical outlets, circuit breakers, high voltage power lines, sub-stations, etc.

The Earth emits a naturally occurring magnetic field all around us and has an effect on paranormal activity. Geo-magnetic storm activity can also have a great influence on paranormal activity. For more information on this kind of phenomena visit: www.noaa.sec.com.

There are many different types of EMF meters; and each one, although it measures with the same unit of measurement, may react differently. An EMF meter can range from anywhere to $12 to $1,000 or more depending on the quality and features that it has. Most meters are measuring the AC (alternating current, the type of fields created by man-made electricity) fields and some can measure DC (direct current-naturally occurring fields, batteries also fall into the category of DC) fields. The benefit of having a meter that can measure DC fields is that they will automatically filter out the artificial fields created by AC fields and can pick up more naturally occurring electro magnetic fields. Some of the higher-tech EMF meters are so sensitive that they can pick up the fields generated by living beings. The EMF meter was originally designed to measure the earth's magnetic fields and also to measure the fields created by electrical an artificial means.

There have been various studies over the years about the long-term effects of individuals living in or near high fields. There has been much controversy as to whether or not long-term exposure to high fields can lead to cancer. It has been proven though that no matter what, long term exposure to high fields can be harmful to your health. The ability to locate these high fields within a private residence or business is vital to the investigation. We may offer suggestions to the client as to possible solutions for dealing with high fields. The wiring in a home or business can greatly affect the possibility of high fields. If the wiring is old and/ or not shielded correctly, it can emit high fields that may affect the ability to correctly notate any anomalous fields that may be present.

Audio Recording Equipment

Audio recording equipment is used for conducting EVP (Electronic Voice Phenomena) research and experiments. What is an EVP? An EVP is a phenomenon where paranormal voices or sounds can be captured with audio recording devices. The theory is that the activity will imprint directly onto the device or tape, but has not been proven to be an absolute fact. The use of an external microphone is essential when conducting EVP experiments with analog recording equipment. The internal microphone on an analog tape recorder can pick up the background noise of the working parts within the tape recorder and can taint the evidence as a whole. Most digital recorders are quiet enough to use the internal microphone, but as a general rule of thumb, we do not use them. An external microphone will be used always. Another theory about EVP research is that an authentic EVP will happen within the range 250-400hz. This is a lower frequency range and isn't easily heard by the human ear, and the human voice does not emit in this range. EVP is rarely heard at the moment it happens—it is usually revealed during the playback and analysis portion of the investigation.

Thermometers

The use of a thermometer in an investigation goes without saying. This is how we monitor the temperature changes during the course of an investigation. CCPRS is currently using Digital thermometers with remote sensors as a way to set up a perimeter and to notate any changes in a stationary location of an investigation. The Air-probe thermometer can take "real time" readings that are instantly accurate. This is the more appropriate thermometer for measuring air temperature and "cold spots" that may be caused by the presence of paranormal phenomena. The IR Non-contact thermometer is the most misused thermometer in the field of paranormal research. CCPRS does not own or use IR Non-contact thermometers for this reason. The IR (infra-red) Non-contact thermometer is meant for measuring surface temperatures from a remote location. It shoots an infrared beam out to an object and bounces to the unit and gives the temperature reading. I have seen, first hand, investigators using this thermometer as a way to measure air temperature. NO, this is not correct! Enough said. In an email conversation that I have had with Grant Wilson from TAPS, he has said that, "Any change in temperature that can't be measured with your hand is not worth notating..."

Endnotes

[1]The source of this timeline of Alcatraz was a website that is no longer available online. The website was located at the address www.alcatraz.cc.

[2]The source of this timeline of the military history of Alcatraz was the National Park Service. The original was accessed in May 2007 online at http://www.nps.gov/archive/alcatraz/miltime.html.

[3]The film that depicted (quite inaccurately) the life of Henri Young was "Murder in the First" (1995).

[4]The movie was "Birdman of Alcatraz," which was filmed in 1962.

Bibliography

Alcatraz Hauntings. Famous Ghost Stories. Your Ghost Stories. Retrieved June 6, 2007 from http://www.yourghoststories.com/famous-ghost-stories/alcatraz-hauntings.php.

"Alcatraz History." *Alcatraz: A Historical Narrative*. Ocean View Publishing. Retrieved March 3, 2007 from http://www.alcatrazhistory.com/.

American Paranormal Investigators. "2003 California Ghost Hunters Conference." Retrieved March 12, 2007 from http://www.ap-investigations.com/Alcatraz_2003.

Babyak, Jolene. *Eyewitness on Alcatraz: Life on THE ROCK as told by the Guards, Families & Prisoners*. Berkeley, California: Ariel Vamp Press, 1988.

Baron, Carla. "Carla Baron Home Page." Retrieved July 15, 2007 from http://home.att.net/~carla.baron/mainpage.html.

Betty (2006). Alcatraz. "Real Haunted Houses user comments forum." Retrieved March 24, 2007 from http://www.realhaunts.com/united-states/alcatraz/.

Chicago Historical Society (1999). "History Files: Al Capone." Retrieved July 1, 2007 from http://www.chicagohs.org/history/capone.html.

Dwyer, Jeff. *Ghost Hunter's Guide to the San Francisco Bay Area*. Gretna, Louisiana: Pelican Publishing Company, 2005.

Eagle, Adam. *Alcatraz! Alcatraz! The Indian Occupation of 1969–1971*. Berkeley, California: Heyday Books, 1992.

GAzis-Sax, Joel. (1996). *Henri Young, 244-AZ. Alcatraz: The Warden Johnston Years 1933–1948*. Retrieved July 10, 2007 from http://www.notfrisco2.com/alcatraz/bios/hyoung/hyoung4.html.

GAzis-Sax, Joel. (1997). Joe Bowers (Josef Ebner) 210 AZ. *Alcatraz: The Warden Johnston Years 1933–1948*. Retrieved July 10, 2007 from http://www.notfrisco2.com/alcatraz/bios/bowers/.

"Ghost In My Suitcase (2001–2006)." *Alcatraz: The Rock*. 23 House Publishing. Retrieved March 6, 2007 from http://www.ghostinmysuitcase.com/places/alcatraz/index.htm.

Ghost Trackers (2004). Ghost Trackers on DF's Return to Alcatraz. "Ghost Trackers Comment Forum." The Carla Baron Connection. Retrieved April 3, 2007 from http://www.carlabaron.net/forum/showthread.php?t=16.

Gregory, George. *Alcatraz Screw: My Years as a Guard in America's Most Notorious Prison*. Columbia and London: University of Missouri Press, 2002.

Heaney, Frank. *Inside the Walls of Alcatraz by Frank Heaney, Alcatraz's Youngest Guard*. Palo Alto, California: Bull Publishing Company, 1987.

Katie (2005). Alcatraz. "Real Haunted Houses user comments forum." Retrieved March 24, 2007 from http://www.realhaunts.com/united-states/alcatraz/.

Kelly, Bill. *Homicidal Mania: The Fifteen Most Horrific Cases Ever to Shock America*. Bonus Chapter. Cybersleuths Home Page. Retrieved July 3, 2007 from http://www.cybersleuths.com/billkelly/bkbonuschap1.htm.

Kouri, Michael. "Michael J. Kouri Home Page." Retrieved July 17, 2007 from http://icghosts.homestead.com/Books.html.

Laura (2004). "Cell Block Encounter." *San Diego Paranormal Research Project: Alcatraz*. Retrieved on March 18, 2007 from http://www.sdparanormal.com/page/page/914866.htm.

"Legends of America (2003–2007)." *The History & Hauntings of Alcatraz*. Legends of America: A Travel Site for the Nostalgic and Historic Minded. Retrieved July 13, 2007 from http://www.legendsofamerica.com/CA-Alcatraz4.html.

Norma (2006). Alcatraz. "Real Haunted Houses user comments forum." Retrieved March 24, 2007 from http://www.realhaunts.com/united-states/alcatraz/.

Patrick, Kelli. (2005). *Alcatraz*. Paranormal Activity Investigators. Retrieved April 17, 2007 from http://www.ghost-investigators.com/Stories/view_story.php?story_num=28.

Public Broadcasting Service (PBS) (2002). "Timeline of Indian Activism." *Alcatraz Is Not An Island*. Retrieved June 6, 2007 from http://www.pbs.org/itvs/alcatrazisnotanisland/timeline.html.

Smith, Barbara. "Spirits of Alcatraz." *Haunted San Francisco: Ghost Stories from the City's Past by Rand Richards*. San Francisco, California: Heritage House Publishers, 2004.

Snyder, Michael. (2006). "A Personal Experience at Alcatraz." *Past Lifetimes*. Retrieved July 13, 2007 from http://www.pastlifetimes.net/psychic_phone_readings_ghost_story_queen_mary_ghostsa1.htm.

Taylor, Troy. (2006). "Doing Time for Eternity on the Rock: The Hauntings of Alcatraz." *Ghost of the Prairie: America's Most Haunted Places*. Retrieved April 7, 2007 from http://www.prairieghosts.com/gpalcatraz.html.

Ullman, Chris. (2006). "The Ghosts of Alcatraz." *Past Lifetimes*. Retrieved April 11, 2007 from http://www.pastlifetimes.net/psychic_phone_readings_ghost_story_alcatraz_ghosts.htm.